"If you are doubting your CX initiatives describes a well-researched and clearly t support customers achieve their real goals satisfaction. Read this book if you dare t

Matthew Tod, *Former leader of PWC Custom....*

"At last, a step-by-step guide to delivering real-world revenue from long under-utilised customer experience data. When implemented well Yorgov's approach is proven to noticeably raise customers' experience, positively impact tenure and increase recommendations."

Iain Bell, *Former Director, Client Data Services at Afiniti,*
Director Customer Analytics at Liberty Global, and
Head of Customer Intelligence at BSkyB

"Ivaylo Yorgov's book offers fascinating insights into how to strengthen the bond between you and your customers. It's a 'must read' for managers and CX practitioners who want to ensure that customers remain loyal, even after the sale!"

Michael Brandt, *CCXP, Founding Member and Ambassador of*
the European Customer Experience Organization (ECXO),
ex-Group Vice President − Customer Experience at ABB

The New Customer Experience Management

A comprehensive guide to a burgeoning field, this book shows how to design and implement a future-proof post-sales service program focused on proactively addressing customers' needs in a personalized way. For too long, companies have detached from customers after the moment of purchase and done post-sales service in a way that is reactive, generic, and not scalable.

Empowered by the boom in data availability and analytics, future-ready companies will offer their customers proactive personalized post-sales service and reap tangible benefits, including higher customer satisfaction and retention and less negative word of mouth – leading to increased sales and customer lifetime value. As the stories in this book demonstrate, companies like Amazon, Adobe, Garmin, and Liberty Global are leading the way, but companies do not have to be global giants to capitalize on the techniques presented in this guide. To excel at customer experience (CX) management, companies need to implement the best customer feedback and data collection and management practices, develop state-of-the-art analytical models, and have the willingness to act.

This book's strong vision and actionable roadmap, illustrated with real-life success stories, make this a compelling read for CX and customer analytics leaders, practitioners, and students alike.

Ivaylo Yorgov is an award-winning customer experience and analytics leader with more than 15 years of experience. He is currently the Managing Director of GemSeek, a customer analytics company, helping his teams to support clients such as Philips, Liberty Global, Yara, Rockfon, Vodafone, Heidelberg Cement, and Signify.

The New Customer Experience Management

Why and How the Companies of the Future Address Their Customers' Needs Proactively

Ivaylo Yorgov

Routledge
Taylor & Francis Group

NEW YORK AND LONDON

Cover image: © Shutterstock

First published 2023
by Routledge
605 Third Avenue, New York, NY 10158

and by Routledge
4 Park Square, Milton Park, Abingdon, Oxon, OX14 4RN

Routledge is an imprint of the Taylor & Francis Group, an informa business

Library of Congress Cataloging-in-Publication Data
Names: Yorgov, Ivaylo, author.
Title: The new customer experience management : why and how the companies
of the future address their customers' needs proactively / Ivaylo Yorgov.
Description: 1 Edition. | New York, NY : Routledge, 2023. |
Includes bibliographical references and index. |
Identifiers: LCCN 2022023944 (print) |
LCCN 2022023945 (ebook) | ISBN 9781032313443 (hardback) |
ISBN 9781032313412 (paperback) | ISBN 9781003309284 (ebook)
Subjects: LCSH: Customer services. |
Customer relations–Management. | Selling.
Classification: LCC HF5415.5 .Y67 2023 (print) |
LCC HF5415.5 (ebook) | DDC 658.8/12–dc23/eng/20220728
LC record available at https://lccn.loc.gov/2022023944
LC ebook record available at https://lccn.loc.gov/2022023945

ISBN: 9781032313443 (hbk)
ISBN: 9781032313412 (pbk)
ISBN: 9781003309284 (ebk)

DOI: 10.4324/9781003309284

Typeset in Bembo
by Newgen Publishing UK

Contents

Foreword

"He who gives when he is asked has waited too long."
(Lucius Annaeus Seneca)

When people ask me what I do, I often struggle to come up with a snappy answer.

I could say that I am a writer. I could say that I am a researcher. I could say that I am an agitator. I could say that I am an advisor. None of those on their own would be sufficient as I do all of those things, particularly in customer service and experience.

As a result, I tend to default to describing what I am most interested in and what I try to bring about. In short: How do we create organizations that produce better outcomes for both their customers and their people?

This is a space that I have spent the last 25 years in. Initially, I was involved in building and developing businesses and ventures that had customer and employee value at their hearts. But, over the last 14 years, I've been researching, podcasting, blogging, writing, and generally advocating for these better outcomes and advising a few companies along the way to help them elevate their own service and experience outcomes.

Now, while I have written four different books on customer service and experience over the last decade or so, this is the first foreword I have ever written.

I know Gemseek having done some work with them over the last couple of years, so when Mila, one of Ivo's colleagues, approached me and asked if I would consider writing the foreword, I was automatically interested.

My interest grew when I read the manuscript and learned that Ivo's book is built around a central framework called Proactive Personalized Post-Sales Service (PPPS).

The title of the framework, in particular, caught my eye as it talks about both proactive service and personalization. These are two of my favorite drums to bang on.

On proactivity, whilst we have always had the ability to be more proactive, the default position in customer service has always been reactive, i.e., we wait until there is a problem, then do what we can to solve it.

Despite advances in data capture and technology, that is still largely the case.

But, customer expectations are changing all of the time and are only going one way. Up.

And that includes how they view problems: They don't like them and want to be helped proactively to avoid them.

That's not new.

In *How To Wow*, published in 2016, I quoted research conducted by inContact in 2013 (subsequently acquired by Nice) that found that 87% of customers surveyed said they wanted to be contacted proactively by a company when it came to customer service issues. Moreover, they also found that nearly three quarters (73%) of those who had been contacted proactively and had a positive experience said that it led to a positive change in their perception of the business that contacted them.

That research came out nearly ten years ago, and there is little to suggest that things have changed.

Yet, customers still yearn for proactive service.

Similarly, personalization is something we have talked about for a long time now but continue to fail to deliver on. This is despite the fact that overwhelmingly companies and customers both agree that personalized experiences are desired and, if delivered well, would drive improved business results and engagement.

But, NTT's 2021 Global Customer Experience Benchmarking report highlighted a problem at the heart of many personalization efforts. Their report warned that "organisations and consumers have different views of what personalisation means", with consumers saying that personalization is "not about how well the organisation knows them, but how well the organisation is listening to them, and how efficiently and effectively they respond to needs".

The NTT report went on to say that

> Consumers are more interested in being able to choose how they engage with organisations – and having those choices respected – than receiving what organisations think are helpful reminders, or proactive offerings in an attempt to upsell or cross-sell to them. They're also wary about sharing personal data so companies can send them personalised information.

So, while there might be an acknowledgment of the importance of personalization on both sides, there seems to be a lack of a shared understanding of what personalization really means, which is one of the main impediments to achieving more success.

Yet, like in the case of proactive service, customers still desire personalized experiences.

So, what is going on?

Research suggests that one of the primary reasons most businesses fail at these types of initiatives can be put down to how they are organized, run, and measured.

But, leading companies know that in order to compete, differentiate themselves, and drive their businesses forward, they must do what it takes to implement proactive and personalized customer service and experience strategies. Doing so will allow them to lower costs, drive additional revenue, improve satisfaction and NPS scores, increase customer engagement, and boost customer loyalty and retention.

I've been advocating for more proactive and personalized service and experience for over ten years now, so what's really exciting about Ivo's book is that it offers a systematic roadmap to allow firms to overcome these barriers and push forward with the development and implementation of these types of strategies.

Doing so will allow them to build trust and engagement internally (across functions and departments) and externally (with customers) so that both the organization and the customer benefit.

I hope that many companies and leaders buy Ivo's book, and I look forward to seeing more and more examples of valuable and innovative proactive, personalized, post-sale service in the coming years.

Customers are waiting.

Adrian Swinscoe
Customer experience advisor, author, speaker, workshop leader, and aspirant punk at Punk CX. Founding Member and Ambassador of the European Customer Experience Organization (ECXO)
Edinburgh, March 2022

Introduction

Value is not created when a customer buys a product or a service. Value is created when customers improve their well-being by putting the tools they buy to good use.

This, I believe, is the biggest disconnect between a company's interests and that of a customer.

Commercial organizations exist to generate profit; profit comes from selling something at a higher cost than the cost required to produce or deliver it.

Customers want to profit from the transaction as well. They buy things to increase their well-being, whichever way we define it (and we are not in a position to judge whether it's the right thing for them to do).

The difference is that a company puts in most of the work before selling the product. The research and development, marketing, manufacturing, distribution, and the other activities that bring the product or the service from an idea to an actual proposition happen before a customer pays for the product. Alternatively, a customer invests a lot in improving their well-being, i.e., realizing value, after purchasing the product or service.

This creates an imbalance in focus. Following the logic mentioned above, companies prioritize pre-sales and sales. However, for customers, post-sales matter the most. This is aptly visible when we consider the language used to denote the different stages of the process. What happens before and after the sales is expressed by adding a prefix to the main word – sales. The default focus is on sales; what happens before it has the singular purpose of achieving it; what comes later is an afterthought.

Look around your home or your office. Look at the objects that surround you. You have bought these to get a job done. Your shirt or skirt – may be purely functional – to maintain decency and not run around naked; maybe to show intellectual prowess; maybe to look attractive; perhaps to show your partner that you appreciate the gift they gave you for your birthday. Your hairstyle – a statement of your individuality? An inconvenience to take care of daily? A way to attract attention?

I'm sitting in my kitchen right now. Around me: a refrigerator, an oven, a microwave, a steam cooker, a blender, a popcorn maker, and a coffee machine.

DOI: 10.4324/9781003309284-1

Every morning, I have coffee at home; if I work from home, I'd have a second one in the afternoon. Twice daily, this pressure-inducing device allows me to refresh, invigorate, and enjoy the taste of coffee. I've had it for five years now, and back then, it cost me about one hundred euros. How often have I used my popcorn maker, which cost about 25 euro, I wonder? Twice, the last time was three months ago. My steam cooker, with a price tag of two hundred euro? A total of four times, the most recent was over six months ago.

If we measure value as something that is exchanged, then my steam cooker is the highest value-adding product of the three and probably the one from which the producer made the most profit. Improvement in my well-being? If not zero, then at least suspiciously close to zero. My opinion about steam cookers? Useless dust-gathering machines. My opinion about the brand? Decent, I guess; I know it's not their fault that I'm not using it. Will I repurchase it? Will I recommend it to others? No.

If I measured value as something that brings an improvement to my life, then my coffee maker rocks. Given the number of cups I've made with it, the price of one is probably by now quickly approaching zero. So, I love coffee, and I have it at almost no cost by using my coffee maker – what a fantastic deal. And am I impressed by the longevity of this thing! I've wanted to get a new one for the last two or three years now, but the one I own refuses to break and alleviate my anxiety of spending money on things I don't need. If it has one fault, it is this one.

I have worked with clients in the customer experience (CX) domain for over 15 years; sifting through piles of academic research, I've come to believe that companies are missing an opportunity here. A well-designed and executed post-sales program[1] can significantly decrease a company's churn rate, the number of customers spreading negative word-of-mouth, and the number of inbound service calls. It can also boost customers' repeat purchase intentions.

Companies can do several things to support customers in their value-creation efforts once the purchase has been realized. I suggest that we group them into three categories: (1) product/service improvements at large, (2) boosting value-creation, and (3) removing barriers to value-creation.

Companies are always searching for ways to improve their offerings. However, it has received ample attention already, so we will not focus on it here. Of more interest are the other two elements, which, if my experience as a professional and as a customer is of any relevance, companies often overlook.

Value-creation boost initiatives typically revolve around three things: inspiring customers to do more with the product or service, motivating them to do so, and educating them on how to do it. Barrier-removing initiatives are related to making adjustments on the fly or offering improvements or corrections to their products and services after the customer has purchased them.

Both areas have been along for a long time now, of course. Yet, I believe the time is ripe for companies to reconfigure how they do them by making the most of the data at their disposal and the boom in artificial intelligence (AI)/

machine-learning capabilities. These unlock a very specific way of delivering post-sales service — doing it in a proactive and personalized fashion and at scale. This mode of post-sales service delivers the benefits outlined above and is where the leading companies are headed.

Offering proactive personalized post-sales service (PPPS in the remainder of the book) means that you no longer need to wait for a customer to complain to you or reply to a customer's feedback survey to address their potential dissatisfaction. You can act preemptively to mitigate any events that might be preventing the customer from creating value. In addition, you can also boost customers' value-creation efforts proactively. This is not to be equated with cross-selling, way too often, sales efforts get masked under the disguise of supporting the customer.

Offering personalized post-sales service means adjusting your response to the specific needs of the particular customer. It doesn't mean that you need to make your full portfolio of products or services customizable. Personalization, the way I'm using the term here, simply means that you address customers in the way they prefer and when they prefer. If you are trying to boost their value-creation efforts, you do it based on the customers' level of expertise and motivation instead of bombarding everyone with generic advice.

Finally, the key issue is not how to do post-sales in a proactive and personalized fashion but how to do it at scale. This requires having information about potential barriers and appropriate boosts in the value-creation process for every customer. The advancements in data availability, management, and analytics render this possible. I have received many industry awards from my colleagues for developing algorithms to predict customer satisfaction (measured with Net Promoter Score™ - NPS®)[2]: algorithms that yielded a return on investment of 500%.

The remainder of this book follows the structure of this introduction. In the first section, we will discuss the foundations of PPPS. Chapter 1 deals with the theory behind PPPS and introduces a paradigm of thinking that has greatly impacted the book's development, the Service-Dominant Logic (S-DL) of marketing. We will also have a more detailed look at the implications of S-DL for businesses and give examples of initiatives that boost value-creation and those aimed to remove barriers.

Chapter 2 introduces PPPS and its core elements — proactivity, personalization, and scalability. We will talk about why these are the three fundamental aspects of post-sales service of the future and support this with sound academic research. We will close this chapter by giving examples of companies already doing PPPS.

Chapter 3 gives a detailed look at the current barriers to PPPS that companies face. As we'll see, there are many instruments and initiatives organizations can and do employ to deliver post-sales services. However, they are either reactive, generic, not scalable, or a combination of these.

In the second section of this book, we will present a roadmap for designing and implementing PPPS. By necessity, this section is technical in parts, despite my best efforts to keep it as accessible as possible. You might also find the description of the processes and intricacies of the data collection, management, and analytics tedious at times. Yet, I decided that these discussions are needed to show that doing PPPS is an achievable goal.

Chapter 4 kick-starts the process and introduces the roadmap for designing and implementing PPPS. Chapters 5–10 deal with the different phases of the roadmap, with each chapter separated in two – first, we discuss the purpose of this stage and the criteria for success. Second, we discuss how to get there.

Chapter 5 explains how to ensure the successful start of your PPPS program; specifically, we discuss ideas for getting buy-in from the people its execution depends on, and we talk about goal setting. In Chapter 6, we show how to collect the first piece of the puzzle – customer feedback data. Chapter 7 then offers advice on getting the second foundational data element of PPPS – customer data. Chapter 8 examines the data to understand what customers think of your company, its products and services, and why they think it.

In Chapter 9, we utilize what we learned so far and boost the customers' value-creation process or remove barriers. Once we know which actions work and which don't, we turn to Chapter 10, where we will finalize the process by expanding your knowledge to your full customer base. I will also share a fully developed real-life case study describing the work that my team and I did for a client.

In the last chapter in the second section of the book, we briefly discuss the potential challenges one may face in this process. We will also discuss them as we go along, but this chapter offers a different perspective – we'll see the types of challenges you might encounter from customers.

I hope that you will enjoy the journey and, perhaps more importantly, that you will be inspired to explore further the ideas and techniques that underpin PPPS. Knowledge and concepts are only alive when they are put to use. I will be happy knowing that the concepts we will discuss in the following chapters sparked insightful conversations and intellectual explorations. With this, it is time to move on to perhaps the most conceptual chapter – laying the foundations of PPPS.

Notes

1 I'm keeping the name for simplicity. In an ideal world, I'd be calling this value-creation process, as this is what it is – the moment customers actually start producing outputs with the product or the service.

2 Net Promoter®, NPS®, NPS Prism®, and the NPS-related emoticons are registered trademarks of Bain & Company, Inc., Satmetrix Systems, Inc., and Fred Reichheld. Net Promoter Score[SM] and Net Promoter System[SM] are service marks of Bain & Company, Inc., Satmetrix Systems, Inc., and Fred Reichheld.

Section 1

The Foundations of Proactive Personalized Post-Sales Service (PPPS)

How to decrease churn? How to differentiate from your competitors? How to keep up the business momentum? Such questions keep millions of managers up every night, and for a good reason, as answering them is essential for the survival of any company.

To get to the correct answers, we need to look at a couple of other questions beforehand. Why do companies exist? Why does your company exist? Why do people exchange money for products and services daily? If we don't ask these questions, we will be left with scattered and partial answers at best.

The first section of this book lays out the foundations of the proactive personalized post-sales service framework, introduces the theory that underpins it, and describes its main components – the simultaneous focus on post-sales service, proactivity, personalization, and scalability.

DOI: 10.4324/9781003309284-2

1 Value-Creation

A Framework for Marketing

Having defined post-sales service as a critical part of the customer journey in which companies can, but often don't, stay close to their customers to help them create more value, this chapter then describes what actions companies can take to do this. It identifies the initiatives companies can undertake and groups them in four areas: businesses can inspire, motivate, and educate customers and make adjustments in the delivery of their products and services on the fly.

Post-Sales Service Is Imperative for Value-Creation

At the foundation of the proactive personalized post-sales service (PPPS) framework lies the idea that people exchange one type of resource (typically money) for another (goods or services) if and when they value the latter higher than the former,[1] and they cannot produce it themselves.

Both of these are evident in our daily lives. If I can get everything I need by doing it myself, there would be little incentive to engage in any economic exchange. However, such self-sustaining units do not exist, at least at scale, in the world that we live in if they ever did at all. The major driver behind this is specialization. Perhaps it is viable to think that a small group of people, say 100 or 150, can indeed produce everything they need to survive and maybe thrive. However, as groups grow, this economic organization where the tribe does things together and shares all the resources becomes less viable. Naturally, specialization based on knowledge, skills, and competencies, on the one hand, and in the latter stages – of resource ownership – starts to develop. This specialization by activity means that I can no longer do everything myself. To get the knowledge to specialize in something, I need to spend more time doing this thing, meaning that I'm not gaining the skills required to do something else, and I don't have the time for it. On the positive side, I can become more effective at what I'm doing. So, what we have at this point is me, a very good, say, carpenter, and you, a very good apple maker. I need apples, and you need a roof; you do apples, I do roofs. Logically, we begin to exchange one for the other.

Specialization begets further specialization. As I start to do more of what I'm good at, two things will happen. First, I'll gain more knowledge in my

DOI: 10.4324/9781003309284-3

domain. Second, other people will do the same. That is, now I will have competition in my roof-making activities. To retain the opportunity to exchange apples for roof building, I will have to offer better roofs than my competitor. Therefore, I need to spend more time developing in this domain; consequently, I can spend less time and resources on other activities. What happens is that each of us specializes further. To some extent, this is the state of all economies in the world right now – you and I can't do it all by ourselves, so we need to engage in economic exchange.

Let's continue the apple maker example for just a bit longer. On any given day, if I'm a good apple maker, I'd have a certain number of apples in storage. At the same time, other people have specialized in their respective areas and have accumulated certain products or can produce them on demand. The question is, how do we decide what we give and what we get in return? Why would I exchange apples for a roof repair and not for, say, cattle?

The premise that underpins PPPS is that people exchange one thing for another only if they value what they receive more than what they give. I'm not saying people would necessarily be happy with what they are getting. Indeed, some commodities have very inelastic prices. Water and electricity are good examples; we might not be happy with the quality we are getting from the specific company we are buying these from; yet, we also don't have an option. We value water and electricity far more than many of the other goods that we use. In these cases, the principle holds that for voluntary exchange to happen, there must be something of value for both sides. The same goes even in regulated exchanges, such as paying taxes in exchange for public goods like roads and security. Whenever we pay taxes, we state that we value our freedom higher than the amount of money payable in taxes.[2]

So, we are bound to exchange with others, and for voluntary exchange to happen, we must value what we get more than what we give. Going deeper, the next logical questions are, who determines the value of something and how is value created.

To answer these, we will turn to the paradigm-shifting perspective suggested by what is known in marketing as the Service-Dominant Logic (S-DL). The S-DL model was developed by Robert Lusch and Stephen Vargo and later enriched and applied by many others; as a backlash against the model of economic exchange, they were called Goods-Dominant Logic (G-DL).

The G-DL,

> …views the production and exchange of goods as the central components of business and economics. That is, it frames the purpose of the firm and the function of economic exchange in terms of making and distributing products – units of output, usually tangible. It is closely aligned with neoclassical economics, which views actors as rational, firms as profit-maximizing, customers as utility-maximizing, information and resources as flowing easily among economic actors, and markets as equilibrium-seeking… .
>
> (Lusch & Vargo, 2014, 4–5)

As Lusch and Vargo show, G-DL focuses our attention toward three "centricities": goods, the firm, and exchange value. In this model, now challenged by a plethora of social scientists and practitioners, firms are the proactive actors in value-creation; value is created when people and firms engage in an exchange (surplus value); and the focus is on the product, instead of on the end result of this very product.

S-DL challenges these assumptions and proposes a new, more realistic way of seeing economic exchange. It is based on four axioms, which give rise to a further six premises; together, these ten propositions serve as the foundational premises (FPs) of the paradigm. They are as follows[3]:

1   Axiom 1 and FP 1: Service is the fundamental basis of exchange
    S-DL uses as one of its starting points the resources actors (consumers, businesses, even nations) to "create beneficial effects by acting on other resources" (Lusch & Vargo, 2014, 57–58). As actors become increasingly proficient in using the resources they have at their disposal, they specialize, and with specialization comes the need for exchange, as we discussed above.

    The critical difference between the G-DL and the S-DL is the item that is being exchanged. In the former, the output from performing specialized activities is being exchanged; the latter, S-DL, in contrast, "… suggests that the performance of the specialized activities (i.e., the application of operant resources)"[4] (Lusch & Vargo, 2014, 58) is what actors, i.e., people and companies, exchange.

    In the S-DL, goods are merely vehicles for delivering a service in a more scalable or efficient way, but what is hidden beneath the surface of the money-for-goods exchange is an exchange of services, hence the use of the word 'service' in its name. At the bottom of all that we trade lies our operant resources, which we combine in specific ways and apply

> for the benefit of another actor or oneself. It can be provided directly (e.g., a haircut) to other actors or indirectly, either through a good (e.g., personal transportation service through a car), with the good serving as an appliance or distribution mechanism for service, or through a currency
>
> (Lusch & Vargo, 2014, 56)

All that we do is service; goods are mere vehicles for more optimal or scalable delivery. This leads us to the second FP:

2   FP2: Indirect exchange masks the fundamental basis of exchange
    This second premise of S-DL follows directly from the first one. If all economic exchange is ultimately an exchange of services, why is this not more visible? Why do we not know it? Why do we keep talking in G-DL terms?

    What masks this fundamental basis of exchange, according to S-DL, is the indirect nature of all exchanges – the fact that there are various intermediaries between two actors (people or companies). As Lusch and Vargo pointed out, all societies "…move toward creating goods, organizations, and money to assist them in service exchange". (Lusch & Vargo, 2014, 60) These three – goods, organizations, and money – are a form of scaling up economic exchanges between people, making it possible to move from a single person to person exchange, to a company to many customers, or company to company exchange.

Organizations comprise people who coordinate their skills and knowledge (operant resources) and add operand resources (raw materials) to produce a good or service. On the other hand, goods are merely vehicles for service delivery – what could have been delivered by a service is now scaled up and delivered as a good. I can cook for you, or I can give you a multicooker so you can do it yourself; this is how the logic of service-to-goods transformation works. And lastly, instead of exchanging products for products, most societies nowadays engage in money-to-product/service exchange. To keep it simple, we pay for things with money. However, what stands behind money is other services that you or I have delivered. In buying this book, you are investing part of the services that you have provided as a marketing manager, customer experience (CX) leader, or a contact center director, for example. The service logic of all exchanges flows below the surface of these intermediaries we have created to support us in these exchanges.

3 FP3: Goods are distribution mechanisms for service provision

We already hinted at this conclusion when we spoke about axiom 1, but it warrants an elaboration. If service-to-service is the fundamental basis of exchange, this leaves us with a burning question: what is the role of goods?

In S-DL, goods (products) transfer knowledge and a "distribution mechanism for applied skills" (Lusch & Vargo, 2014, 64). When one person's knowledge (he service) is applied in a physical matter (paper), we end up with a product (a book), which becomes a vehicle for the service provision. Instead of sharing knowledge by talking, the person can now provide a scalable service. This is what products (goods) are – scalability devices for what would otherwise be a close to exclusive service. They are distribution channels.

4 FP4: Operant resources are the fundamental source of competitive advantage

This FP is critical for the proactive personalized post-sales service framework, as one of its benefits stems directly from it. The question is, what gives companies a competitive edge? What makes one company better than the other?

Following the logic of everything outlined so far, the answer is unequivocal. What creates a competitive advantage is not raw materials but skills and knowledge. As we just saw, S-DL products are understood to be "properly informed matter", i.e., matter enriched by skills and knowledge. What follows from this understanding is that "only those resources that can produce effects can serve as the fundamental source of competitive or strategic advantage and those resources are never solely static operand resources" (Lusch & Vargo, 2014, 65). A piece of clay means nothing to me, simply because I don't know what to do with it. A piece of clay for a potter is an opportunity to produce a product, be it a work of art or a mundane object. It is not the clay itself that matters; it is what the potter does with it. Admittedly, there are raw materials of different quality. Yet, especially in the world that we live in, in which raw materials have become commoditized, access to good raw material is not the major source of competitive advantage – skills and knowledge are.[5]

5　FP5 states that all economies are service economies. It has less relevance for the topic of interest here, and for brevity's sake, we are simply marking, instead of commenting on it.

6　Axiom 2 and FP 6: The customer is always a co-creator of value
The second axiom of S–DL is absolutely vital for understanding customer experience and, in our case, of post-sales service. In the G–DL, companies create value, and, somewhat ironically, this value is destroyed in the consumption process. In this paradigm, "the value is embedded during production and distribution/marketing without the involvement of the actor who will become the beneficiary of the enterprise's offering" (Lusch & Vargo, 2014, 69). The concept of added value exemplifies this kind of thinking well. This additional value is thought of as something on top of the raw materials that go into production – a company gets wood, iron, nails, hammers, etc., invests efforts and knowledge into them, and produces something new. The creation of value is thus this process of production in which raw materials are transformed into a product.

A different view emerges from the S–DL perspective. Lusch and Vargo considered value to be a "…benefit, an increase in the well-being of a particular actor" (Lusch & Vargo, 2014, 57) and is 'phenomenologically determined', i.e., the value of something can only be judged by its benefactor.

The most important moment to note here is that value is actually not created until the benefactor has benefited from the product or service. Clearly, and more easily visible in the case of products, value is only created when someone is using the products or services. The product themselves have no value if no one is using them. "The value-creation process", Lusch and Vargo continued,

> …does not end with the sale and distribution of the product offering to the actor as beneficiary; rather, the beneficiary actor continues the process of "producing". Stated alternatively, production does not end with manufacturing and distribution; rather, these are intermediary processes. As noted, goods are appliances that provide service for and in conjunction with the beneficiary actor. However, for this service to be delivered, the beneficiary must learn to use,

maintain, repair, and adapt the appliance to their unique needs, usage situation, and behaviors. In summary, in using a product, the beneficiary continues the marketing, value-creation, and delivery process. Cocreation of value thus recognizes that value is always created in the use and integration of resources.

(Lusch & Vargo, 2014, 70)

We can come with thousands of examples from our daily lives. A car manufacturer does not create value when they put together the car. The value – transportation – is created if and only when you and I drive the car. My steam cooker does not create value sitting on my kitchen counter; had I used it more than twice, it would have created value, but it hadn't yet. And running shoes don't create value either – running does.

The same goes with services, albeit in a bit more veiled fashion, as part of the value is created at the moment of sales because this is when usage happens. A haircut, for example, does have value the moment I get it. More importantly, what I might be expecting to get from it is to look smart, trendy, or fashionable. If I don't know how to maintain my haircut, it will not create this value. Same with water; it is easy to see that you and I drink water when we are thirsty, so it might seem that this is where the value of water lies. This is only partially true. We are thirsty because this is the way our bodies tell us that we need water to stay alive, i.e., the value of water is keeping us alive. From this perspective, tap water that is unsafe to drink might seem to be delivering value when I drink it – I'm no longer thirsty – while in fact it might be destroying value by making me ill.

We can continue on and on, but I believe the point is already quite clear. Value, thought of as an improvement to people's lives, can never be created when I buy a product or a service. Value is always created in an interaction between the benefactor and the product or service. More precisely, given that all products or services are services (in a sense, S–DL uses the term), value is always co-created between the benefactor and the company, potentially via intermediaries like products.

7   FP7: The enterprise cannot deliver value but can only offer value propositions

The seventh FP of S–DL follows logically from axiom 2. If value is created at the customer's end, companies cannot provide value themselves. Instead, they can offer the possibility or the tools for creating value. The moment at which companies think they are delivering value – typically, at the moment of sales – what companies are actually doing is unlocking the potential for value-creation; value itself will be created by the customer with the product or service the company has produced or delivered. This is very easily seen in educational systems of any kind. A teacher cannot deliver value themselves. If we assume that value, in this case, is a skill or knowledge that the student learns. The student is doing the learning, with the teacher merely providing the service via vehicles like books and lectures.

8   FP8: A service-centered view is inherently customer-oriented and relational

By definition, the traditional, G-DL sees the customer as external to the company and the value delivery process. Therefore, businesses should be encouraged to be customer-oriented – the customer is not an inherent part of the value-creation process. On the other hand, in the S-DL, the customer, being the ultimate creator of value, is an indispensable part of the ecosystem. Companies operating under the S-DL have no choice but to be customer-oriented. Simply put, the customer is where the value is created.

The relational nature of the S-DL stems from the view that value is

> emerging and unfolding over time, rather than as a discrete, production–consumption event. This unfolding, cocreational (directly or through goods) nature of value is relational in the sense that the activities of exchange actors and those of other actors interactively and interdependently combine, over time, to co-create value.
>
> (Lusch & Vargo, 2014, 73)

How much value I create with the products or services I have does not depend solely on the one specific product that your company manufactures. Instead, it depends on the specific combination of a myriad of other products I possess, other value propositions, and the skills and knowledge I have. However, none of these is enough on its own to create value. I only get to create value through the interaction of these different elements. This logically leads to the ninth FP of S-DL.

9   Axiom 3 and FP 9: All economic and social actors are resource integrators

From an S-DL point of view, markets are unbounded "because the extent of resource integration by human actors is unlimited and, in fact, ever-expanding because the more resources that are integrated, the more resources there are to integrate" (Lusch & Vargo, 2014, 77). In their daily lives, you and I included, people acquire, integrate, and operate many resources to 'increase their well-being.' For example, as a customer, I am not in the market for haircuts; I am in the market of looking good, smart, trendy, or whatever else I choose. To achieve this, I can get a new haircut; I can also buy new sneakers, change the type of music I listen to, and start going to the trendy places in the city. A haircut is rarely enough; customers need to orchestrate all the resources at their disposal to develop a holistic and coherent identity. This way of seeing markets unlocks tremendous opportunities for offering what, for clarity, I'll call adjacent products or services; from a customer perspective, they could very well not be adjacent but core ones.

10   Axiom 4 and FP 10: Value is always uniquely and phenomenologically
      determined by the beneficiary
      Axiom 4 of S-DL places emphasis on two things. On the one hand,
      how much value is created is a judgment only the beneficiary can make.
      To put it bluntly, it does not matter what other actors in the ecosystem
      think – what matters is how much the beneficiary values what is being
      exchanged. It also points to the contextual nature of value, by stating that

> every incidence of service exchange creates a different experience
> and unique (to the beneficiary) instance and assessment of value.
> This is because each instance takes place in a different context,
> involving the availability, integration, and use of a different combin-
> ation of resources and actors. These results have a differential impact
> on the viability of a system (actor), which is uniquely assessed by
> the beneficiary.
>
> (Lusch & Vargo, 2014, 78)

When thinking about the value proposition they want to offer, companies, following this logic, have to think about specific instances in
which customers will use the product or service. This is already a perspective adopted by many businesses. Yet, it warrants a repetition as seen
from the customer's perspectives; many products and services are still not
designed this way, or at the very least haven't reached the full potential
offered by this perspective.

In summary (also refer to Table 1.1), our discussion on value so far
outlines that we have no choice but to engage in economic exchanges
with other actors because of specialization. We can't get everything we
need and want on our own, so we trade with others. What we are exchanging between ourselves is the application of specialized skills and knowledge, and they "can be transferred (1) directly, (2) through education
or training, or (3) indirectly by embedding them in objects" (Vargo &
Lusch, 2004, 9). All of these can be subsumed in the category of 'a service'. The direct and the education and training ways of transfer are
equivalent to what we call services and the indirect one to goods/
products. While these are clearly different ways to transfer knowledge
and skills, they are also in their essence the same thing. They are a service provided by one actor to another. Products, in this sense, are merely
vehicles for service provision.

We need to value what we get more than what we give for voluntary exchanges to occur. In the lens through which we chose to look
at it, value is quite simply an improvement of the well-being of the
benefactor. This is a rather loose definition, yet it has the advantage of
pointing out the phenomenological nature of value – whether something benefits an actor is determined by only the actor.

Value is not embedded in the exchange of services itself but is value-
in-use – it is created during the usage of a product or a service by

Table 1.1 The Premises of Service-Dominant Logic

Premise	Implication
Service is the fundamental basis of exchange	What we exchange between each other is not the output of specialized activities, but the performance of these activities. In other words, a company that produces male groomers is not selling groom**ers**, but groom**ing**.
Indirect exchange masks the fundamental basis of exchange	The fact that service is the fundamental basis of exchange is concealed by the fact that there are various intermediaries between the supplier and the beneficiary of the service.
Goods are distribution mechanisms for service provision	There is no fundamental difference between goods and services – the former are merely vehicles for the indirect and scalable provision of the latter.
Operant resources are the fundamental source of competitive advantage	The skills and knowledge, and not the raw materials, a company puts into the making of a product or the delivery of a service is what gives it a competitive advantage. It is what we do with the raw materials that matter, not the materials themselves.
All economies are service economies	All economic eras or economies are fundamentally service economies. The distinction between a hunger-gatherer economy and an industrial one is a difference in type of specialization, rather than a difference in the principles underpinning it.
The customer is always a co-creator of value	Value is not embedded in the product or the service – it has to be created by the consumer. A product, say, a laptop, has no inherent value for the consumer – it only has value to the extent that they use it to improve their well-being (however defined).
The enterprise cannot deliver value but can only offer value propositions	This follows directly from the previous premise. If value is always co-created by the customer, then companies can only suggest or propose ways to create value, but cannot create it fully on their own.
A service-centered view is inherently customer-oriented and relational	Everything discussed so far puts the customer directly at the core of any business. Customer-centricity is no longer a patch to the value-delivery process, but the very focal point of it.
All economic and social actors are resource integrators	The way customers create value is by integrating multiple resources, of which the product or the service provided by a company is merely a part. To create value with a male groomer, for example, one needs to also have the knowledge and skills to use it. No matter how brilliant the product, value may still not get created if the customer doesn't create it.
Value is always uniquely and phenomenologically determined by the beneficiary	There is no value beyond what the customer considers of value.

an actor. As Vargo and Lusch stated, "the customer still must learn to use, maintain, repair, and adapt the appliance to their unique needs, usage situation, and behaviors. In summary, in using a product, the customer is continuing the marketing, consumption, and value-creation and delivery processes" (Vargo & Lusch, 2004, 11). The customer, in a nutshell, is always a co-creator of value. Seen from this perspective, a "customer's value-creation process can be defined as a series of activities performed by the customer to achieve a particular goal" (Payne et al., 2008, 86), with the company's goal being "one of providing experiential interactions and encounters which customers perceive as helping them utilize their resources" (Payne et al., 2008, 87).

What happens very often, even in today's world in which the insights from S-DL, in one way or another, are known to business leaders, is that companies focus on building the potential for value-creation instead of on realizing this value. The products and services businesses deliver are merely value propositions; they only contain the potential for a customer to create value, but in no way presuppose it. Companies can, and a lot of them are on this path, do much more than this – they can remain involved and help in the process of value-creation far more than they are doing it today.

Because value is value-in-use, and the customer is always a co-creator in the process, somewhat ironically, value-creation begins when companies tend to disengage from the process – after the sales are complete, i.e., at the post-sales service stage of the customer journey. Post-sales (or after-sales) service emerges, in this view, not as an unwanted 'patch' to customer service companies would be happy to get rid of, but as the most critical part of the company–customer interaction. The very term 'post-sales' shows the prevalent way of thinking on the topic. It is a company-centric term that portrays it as something that happens after what, one is led to think, is most important for the company – the sales. For clarity, I'll keep the term 'post-sales' throughout this book; it would be more accurate to call it the 'value-creation' phase of the company–customer interaction.

How Can Companies Support Customers in the Value-Creation Process?

Given everything we discussed so far, what can companies do to support customers in their value-creation efforts? How can businesses help customers generate more value? I believe there are five ways companies can help customers create more value.

1   One of them is related to the value proposition itself. Improvements in the products and services in terms of features, longevity, design, etc. are all things companies can and do to unlock more value-creation opportunities for customers. Every iteration or new model which adds elements or features that help customers create more value fall squarely in

this bucket. This process has received ample attention already, so we'll only briefly touch upon it in this book.

The remaining four ways companies can help customers create more value go beyond the provision of the product or service itself and are related to the post-sales service part of the journey. In addition to improving their products and services, companies can contribute to the value-creation process by:

2   inspiring customers to do more with their value proposition
3   motivating them to do more
4   educating them how to do more
5   offering improvements or corrections to their products and services that improve their performance after the purchase, i.e., make adjustments on the fly

Inspiring Customers

Inspiring customers to do more is akin to encouraging them to adopt a new goal or set a new challenge or show them that the product or service the company delivers can do more than customers initially thought.

This process is results-focused, and the inspiration is about showing how life may look. While inspiration is often used to sell a product or service, it can also be an important part of the post-sales service. One way in which companies inspire customers is by showing them what others have done. This is largely the function of allowing customers to connect and make friends. Seeing what others are doing creates social pressure and gives ideas

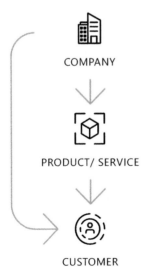

COMPANY

PRODUCT/ SERVICE

CUSTOMER

Product/ Service-related initiatives:
Adjustments on the fly, e.g., customer support, service recovery processes, guarantees.

Customer-related initiatives:
• Inspiration
• Motivation
• Education

Figure 1.1 Initiatives companies can undertake to support customers in the value-creation process.

for things you can do. A subclass of this is working with celebrities who serve as role models. Examples abound Michael Jordan and his cooperation with Nike; Drew Barrymore and Crocs; Georgy Clooney and Nespresso, etc. The goal here is to show a vision of a brighter future (closely tied to the use of the respective product or service).

Motivating Customers

The motivation process often takes the form of calls to action, like "You can do it now!" to use the most obvious example, or of answering the question 'Why?' – What is the customer going to gain if they do xyz? Why is this important?

Also frequently thought of as part of the sales process, motivation is also needed in the post-sales service phase. After all, a vision doesn't just realize itself but requires action on the person's side. In recent years, an increasing number of companies have adopted and applied insights from behavioral economics to do this, with the use of notifications as nudges being perhaps the clearest illustration. For example, Garmin's smartwatches constantly track the number of steps one takes per day. There are two ways in which Garmin tries to encourage users to walk more. The first one offers a push; if you are inactive for a certain amount of time, your Garmin watch would automatically send you a notification and urge you to walk for a bit. The second gives you positive reinforcement by tracking your walking records like most steps in a day or the longest streak of days you have accomplished your steps-goal. Both of these, the push and the pull, motivate us to do more to accomplish our vision and goals.

Educating Customers

Adam Avramescu, one of the thought-leaders in the field of Customer Education, defines it as a "function [that] strategically accelerates account and user growth by changing behaviors, reducing barriers to value, and improving the way people work" (Avramescu, 2019, 13). Once inspired and motivated, we also need to know how to achieve our goal; this applies to all areas of life – from being a good father, mother, brother, or a friend, through our professional lives, to our identities as customers. This, then, is the essence of Customer Education – giving customers the skills, abilities, and processes that allow them to create more value with the product or the service.

Continuing with the Garmin example, their smartwatches also track sleep quality and patterns. Now, things are relatively easy with steps – if I want to accomplish my goal, I just need to walk. With sleep, things can get trickier, as it is not exactly a process over which we have full control. Still, we can do things to improve the quality of our sleep – less coffee, less screen time, etc. – and it is exactly these tips that Garmin offers daily. So, in addition to inspiring us to set a goal, providing the why ("Getting the right amount of sleep is one of the most important things you can do for your health"), and tracking our progress to it, Garmin also helps us get there ("You slept too little, and the overall quality was low. You may feel very tired today. You got a lot of very intense exercise, which impacted your sleep quality. Try to eat well, get plenty of rest, and avoid overexerting yourself in the future".).

Of course, Customer Education can also take much simpler forms, and one needs to look no further than what's included in pretty much any product box to see it. Manuals and tutorials serve exactly this function; their goal is to give us the basics to operate our device. The same goes for frequently asked questions on websites. These initiatives provide education, albeit rudimentary, into the workings of the products, thus helping us as customers to create more value.

The ultimate form education can take is making the product design so good that there is no need for education. This is indeed the logic and the aspiration behind design thinking – good design goes unnoticed; everything happens so smoothly and seamlessly that there is absolutely no effort on our side to start using the product.

Adjustments on the Fly

Last but not least, companies can make adjustments to their products or services in the process of delivering them to customers. Many things can go wrong during the product's usage or the service's output, and these decrease the value customers can create. Companies try to mitigate these adverse effects and restore value to the expected level by doing what in the academic literature is known as 'service recovery', and in the business world, typically goes by customer support or customer service. Contact centers supporting customers by answering their questions and product guarantees promising that if anything goes wrong, the product will be repaired or replaced are examples of adjustments companies make on the fly to continue assisting customers in the value-creation process.

Chapter Summary

The areas we discussed above – customer inspiration, motivation, education, and adjustments on the fly are all, in my humble view, areas that companies have so far underappreciated. To be sure, businesses are not ignorant of these. Yet, the focus of companies' efforts has so far been more on creating the value proposition, convincing customers that it is a compelling one, and bringing it to them, rather than on helping customers create value by walking together with them through the process. Even when companies implement initiatives in these domains, they often suffer from flaws, ranging from lack of scalability through being generic to being reactive.

What I believe we lack is a well-defined vision for how companies can support customers in the value-creation process, or in other words, for how companies can turn post-sales service from a cost center to a (or THE) profit center of the business. Next, we turn our attention to discussing what companies are currently doing and what they can do better in these domains.

Notes

1 Or when they trust the promise a company or another individual makes for a product or a service.
2 Clearly, this is not the full story, but a full-blown discussion on this is far beyond the scope or topic of this book.
3 All premises are based on Lusch and Vargo (2014).
4 Operant resources in S-D Logic are "resources that are capable of acting on other (potential) resources to create benefit; they are often intangible and dynamic. Common examples of operant resources are human skills and capabilities" (Lusch & Vargo, 2014, 57). Operand resources are "(potential) resources that require other resources to act on them to provide benefit. They are static and often tangible, such as natural resources" (Lusch & Vargo, 2014, 57).

References

Avramescu, A. (2019). *Customer education: Why smart companies profit by making customers smarter.* Kindle Edition.

Lusch, R., & Vargo, S. (2014). *Service-dominant logic: Premises, perspectives, possibilities.* Kindle Edition. Cambridge: Cambridge University Press. doi:10.1017/CBO9781139043120

Payne, A. F., Storbacka, K., & Frow, P. (2008). Managing the co-creation of value. *Journal of the Academy of Marketing Science*, 36(1), 83–96. doi:10.1007/s11747-007-0070-0

Vargo, S. L., & Lusch, R. F. (2004). Evolving to a new dominant logic for marketing. *Journal of Marketing*, 68(1), 1–17. doi:10.1509/jmkg.68.1.1.24036

2 The Power of Proactive Personalized Post-Sales Service

I hope that by now you are convinced that post-sales service is not a simple add-on to the product or service your company is providing. Given that this is when the customers create value, you can't detach from the process and just let them do the best they can; I believe this is exactly the right time to be next to your customers.

But what is a company to do in practice? How can you ensure that you are helping customers create value? How would a good post-sales program (or, again, more accurately – value-creation support program) look?

There is a host of insights, academic and real-life, to give us hints, and they all point in this direction: A good post-sales program would allow you to be proactive, personalize your approach, and do it at scale.

Proactive Post-Sales Service

Think for a second about how you are reading this text. Our common sense tells us that the way this happens is that we see ink on paper (or differently colored dots on a screen), we recognize a shape (letters), we connect the shapes into bigger wholes (words) which form even bigger wholes (sentences). This is not an entirely inaccurate description of what's happening.

Indeed, our brains use input from the environment and make sense of it to navigate our bodies in the world. Sensory input, such as of visuals, sounds, touch, or a purely chemical reaction like our sense of smell or taste, gets combined in our brains to form an image of what is around and within our bodies. This input is then used to generate appropriate actions according to our brains. The purpose of these actions is first and foremost to ensure that we survive. It is a primary imperative of all living things to stay alive and, hopefully, well; there is no escape from this biological demand.

From a brain's perspective, the most basic imperative for managing a body is to manage its energy budget. You and I don't have an endless storage of everything our bodies need to survive, like salts, minerals, and carbs. Instead, the way we operate is by getting these on an as-needed basis. When supplies of carbs get low, our brain gets notified and initiates appropriate actions to find and get carbs.

DOI: 10.4324/9781003309284-4

The second thing our brains do to keep our bodies alive from an energy management perspective is to use what's available wisely in the first place. Our muscles and liver store the equivalent of 1.800 to 2.000 calories in the form of glycogen; that is it. Our brains work with this energy supply and navigate our actions to ensure that we don't completely run out of energy and avoid the negative consequences. As to the latter, just talk to someone who has ever run a marathon. In runner's lingo, the dreadful thing called 'hitting the wall' is the exhaustion of these 2.000 calories in the form of glycogen that you and I have in our bodies. It usually occurs around the 30th kilometer, as running burns 60–70 calories per kilometer. The effect is akin to hitting a wall – what your brain starts screaming is, 'Stop! Stop right now!' The reason this happens is that your brain is trying to optimize the use of available resources; energy efficiency is one of the primary imperatives of life, not a modern-day perk of consumer products.

At this point, we need to ask ourselves one question. If our brain's task is first and foremost to keep us alive by managing our energy supply, what's the best way to do it? At the beginning of the chapter, we described the process as input comes first and action second. Intuitive enough, but there is a more efficient method of doing this, and our brains are using it all the time.

Our brains are "prediction machines" (Clark, 2013, 181).

While the processes of perception-making and sense-acting are efficient, there is a better way of doing it. Managing our energy budget, just like our financial budget, is best done proactively, in an anticipatory fashion, and in addition to the commonsense bottom-up process, our brains also apply this less intuitive, top-down approach. The brain doesn't wait for energy to be depleted. Instead, it predicts what will happen and act according to this prediction. The neuroscientist Lisa Feldman Barrett explains:

> When it came to body budgeting, prediction beat reaction. A creature that prepared its movement before the predator struck was more likely to be around tomorrow than a creature that awaited a predator's pounce. Creatures that predicted correctly most of the time, or made nonfatal mistakes and learned from them, did well. Those that frequently predicted poorly, missed threats, or false-alarmed about threats that never materialized didn't do so well. They explored their environment less, foraged less, and were less likely to reproduce.
>
> (Barrett, 2020, 6)[1]

While this doesn't happen all the time, our brains tend to be one step ahead of us in managing our energy budget and avoiding threats. It happens all the time in daily life as well. Online meetings have become the norm since 2020, and most of the conference call applications offer the possibility to blur the background. However, blurred though, one can still glimpse at what is in the background. Interestingly, often times we don't see enough to be certain what we think we are seeing is really what we are seeing. We see a silhouette or a contour, and we tend to assume that this is a vase, and this is a person, and this is a painting. In fact, there is rarely enough to tell us that we are right – our brains fill in the information simply because this is what makes the most sense in this context. And this effect goes much beyond our vision. As de Lange et al. (2018) explain,

> In the sensorimotor domain, predictions of the sensory consequences of our motor commands help us to distinguish external sensations from the mere consequences of our own movements, leading to the well-known fact that we cannot tickle ourselves [149]. In hearing, our brains can "fill in" corrupted syllables in speech with those that are most likely given the context of the surrounding words and sentences [150]. In addition, imagine expecting raisin bread but getting a mouthful of olive bread instead – you probably will not be able to identify what it is you are eating initially.
>
> (de Lange et al., 2018, 765)

The way our brains use these predictions is akin to the way companies try to do it. The purpose of perception and making sense of perception is always to drive action. Consequently, the purpose of predictions about what's happening in the world is to drive preemptive action, or in other words, to be proactive.

Aside from our bodies, this approach can do miracles in the business world and, more specifically, when offering post-sales service. The impact of proactive post-sales service on customer experience (CX) and satisfaction is still an underexplored topic in the academic marketing literature. Still, the vast majority of the studies are unequivocal. Proactive post-sales service delivers better business outcomes than reactive one: it decreases churn, negative word-of-mouth, negative affect, and the number of inbound service calls, and increases customers' perception of the company as being innovative and boosts repeat purchase intentions. Let's have a look at the evidence.

In one of the first explorations of how proactive post-sales service could benefit companies, Retana et al. researched the impact of doing proactive Customer Education on business results. In a field experiment in 2011, they examined the effects of proactively contacting customers of a public cloud infrastructure immediately after signing up on key performance indicators (KPIs) such as churn, the number of questions asked, and service usage. During the two months study, 2,673 customers signed up for the service. Of them, 366 were randomly selected to receive "a short phone call followed up by a support ticket through which the provider offered initial guidance on how to use the basic features of the service" (Retana et al., 2015, 3).

The experiment results provide conclusive evidence of the positive impact of proactively educating customers. On the one hand, those who received a company-initiated call to receive initial guidance were about 3% points less likely to churn in the first week, or a churn rate decrease of close to 50%. Second, these customers also asked approximately 20% fewer questions than the others. This is important, as it allows companies to decrease the costs for "labor-intensive reactive technology support" (Retana et al., 2015, 4). Finally, showing how proactive education helps customers create more value increased the service usage by about 50%. In short, a simple company-initiated phone call after signing up to offer customers initial guidance significantly decreased churn and the number of questions asked and increased their use of the service.

Further evidence for the positive impact of proactive, personalized post-sales service comes from Shin et al, who compared proactive vs. reactive interaction for service failure prevention. They conducted several scenario-based experiments in a retail context (executed via surveys), varying whether the participants received proactive or reactive service. In the proactive case,

> respondents were asked to imagine that they visit a hypothetical electronics store called SAB Electronics to buy a new laptop computer and anti-virus software. At the checkout counter, an employee (referred to by the gender-neutral name "Jaime") tells them about the difficulty of installing the software and offers to install it in the store. Later that evening, the customer in the scenario reads a tech blog that says many consumers have found the anti-virus software installation difficult to perform on their own and should seek assistance from their retailer.
>
> (Shin et al 2017, 172)

In the reactive scenario, customers were not told about the potential issues and had to call the store for support. The results show that proactive support increases customer satisfaction (6.32 vs. 5.33 for reactive) and repurchase intentions (6.27 vs. 5.18 for reactive).

Related to this, Becker et al conducted a field experiment investigating the impact of proactive vs. reactive post-sales service on the number of inbound calls and, more importantly, on immediate churn. Working with a European telecommunications company, they contacted part of its newly acquired customers to offer post-sales service, while the rest (the control group) received no treatment. In the proactive scenario, "…the service agent asked customers for feedback, helped them with optional service features (e.g., setting up the mailbox), and provided information on common pitfalls (e.g., international roaming)—all based on a compulsory script" (Becker et al., 2020, 57). They reported fewer inbound service calls and immediate churn in the proactive condition than the reactive one. Interestingly, proactive post-sales service remained effective even when service agents tried to upsell the customer, albeit less effective than the plain service call with no up-selling.

In service recovery, the importance of being proactive when making adjustments on the fly is offered by a study by Voorhees et al. (2006). The researchers employed a critical incident survey approach, where they collected qualitative and quantitative data. Respondents were asked to describe recent (within the past six months) dissatisfactory service experiences. Specifically, they were asked to describe the events leading up to the service experiences and then explain what happened. Finally, they were asked "to describe both the firms' and their reactions to the encounters. Respondents were then asked to respond to a series of scaled items that assessed repurchase intentions, negative word-of-mouth intentions, negative affect, perceived regret, and a series of control variables" (Voorhees et al., 2006, 517). In total, 530 people were interviewed. Some of them didn't file a complaint to a company about the experience they described; others did, and it was resolved satisfactorily; others did but didn't receive a satisfactory response. We are most interested in the people who didn't complain but received a company-initiated recovery. In full support for proactively addressing customer needs, people who received an organization-initiated recovery exhibited the highest repurchase intention of all other groups. That is, they were more likely to buy again compared to everyone else. In addition, the intention to spread negative word-of-mouth was also lower in this group, albeit at a level similar to those who complained and received a satisfactory recovery.

Finally, in 2019, Trang & Tho reported the results from several surveys which investigated whether companies that provide proactive post-sales service are considered more innovative and if customer satisfaction with them is higher. In two product categories, laptops and cars, the researchers found that customers who thought a company delivered proactive post-sales services were more likely to consider the company as innovative, and they were also more satisfied with the company (with innovativeness mediating the effect).

In sum, the business benefits of providing proactive post-sales services are, putting it moderately, significant. Relatively simple, thus financially non-extensive, initiatives to contact customers proactively decrease churn and customer dissatisfaction and make customers more willing to buy again from the company – all indicators that are the Holy Grail of customer experience management. This does not seem to be news for business leaders. In a 2020 survey by McKinsey, "Nearly two-thirds of respondents ranked the ability to act on CX issues in near real-time as among their top three priorities…" (McKinsey & Company, 2021a). As with many other things, the issue is that knowledge is rarely enough. In the same survey, a mere "13 percent of leaders expressed certainty that their organizations could achieve this level of rapid insight through existing systems" (McKinsey & Company, 2021a). How to achieve it will be the topic of a subsequent chapter. For now, let's turn to the second requirement of a post-sales program that contributes to the process of value-creation by customers – personalization.

Personalized Post-Sales Service

"How do we", a minor character in the liked by some Netflix series "You", asks in a literature workshop, " keep the readers' attention?" In the past, I've been tempted by fiction writing and have read and listened to much advice on the subject. Creating powerful dialogues, building a story arch, or showing the environment are all things every storyteller needs to do to develop a compelling story. But the most concise insight I've ever heard on writing, and storytelling in general, is the answer to the above question: "By making the universal painfully specific". Come to think about it, the stories that have moved me, and I think you'd find it's the same with you, have two key characteristics.

On the one hand, they convey an insight, a new way of looking at the world that enriches my perspective. It could be an observation, an experience, a truth I didn't know, or in most cases – a question; whatever it is, it opens new perspectives and possibilities.

The second thing good stories do is bring this universal insight to the human scale. Every story can be formalized and told as a sequence of fairly standard components. You will always have a hero who embarks on a journey, encounters challenges, and receives help along the way until they meet the ultimate challenge, wins, and returns to the ordinary world with whatever they gain and brings it to the community.

The thing is this is not how stories are told. Instead, specific people embark on specific journeys and face very specific challenges. It's not simply 'the hero' who sets off to overthrow the government in V for Vendetta. It is a man with a mask who lives in a huge underground space full of pieces of art, who also fights really well. It is not simply 'against an authoritarian regime' that he's against. It is against a regime built by a specific person in the UK in the near future, and so on.

This level of specificity makes us relate to the stories simply because they make them more tangible, tactile almost. We can't touch or smell an abstract 'hero', but we can get close to having this sensation when we read about or see a specific person. Similarly, an idea has no materiality, making it difficult to grasp. Blowing up the house of the parliament, to continue the example, becomes very specific; add to this the fact that the hero sets an exact date and time at which he will do it, and you have all the ingredients of an immersive story.

The way personalization works in business life is not unlike in a story where the company is the storyteller, the product or service is the hero, and the audience is the customer. A product or a service delivered without any customization is abstract, universal. It is what every person who pays for it gets. My dryer is the same as yours and as the one of this other person. And the customer service I'll receive when I call the contact center of my telecommunications provider will also be the same; in most cases, there would even be a script for handling me and my questions.

Of course, there are benefits to this approach, like low production costs and a wide reach. The downside is that people don't like abstract heroes, and they want to imagine how the universal truths delivered by stories fit into their lives. A product or a service, just like a story, works best when it is tailored to a specific customer, living in this very specific moment in time and space and having a very specific need or a question. This combination of needs, time, and space creates the basis of personalization as it situates a company's post-sales efforts in the specific context in which a customer will be using what we sell to create value. Without finding a way to embed yourself in this specific context, you cannot truly and fully contribute to this process. Your solutions will always be halfway there, simply because they are either not addressing the exact need or question of a customer, or not addressing it at the right time, or not addressing it in the right way (think, channel, for example).

The importance of personalization is underscored by many sources, from leading consultancies to sound academic research. In fall 2021, McKinsey published the results of their Next in Personalization 2021 survey. Fully 71% of consumers expect personalization, and 76% get frustrated when a company "…shows or recommends [them] things that are not relevant…" (McKinsey & Company, 2021b). This is a huge share of customers – three out of four people demand personalization, and circling back to a point we made earlier – that post-sales service is not cross-selling – three out of four are annoyed when a company puts forward something irrelevant. Let's face it; it is just wasting people's limited time and attention. At the same time, there are significant benefits to be gained by personalization. McKinsey report that 76–78% of customers "are more likely to consider purchasing from brands that personalize" (McKinsey & Company, 2021b), to buy again from these companies, and to spread positive word-of-mouth. Very few other initiatives boost these KPIs as effectively as personalization.

In the academic world, the positive impact of service personalization is supported by several studies. For example, Ball et al. (2006) discovered that

> Personalization increases satisfaction and benevolence trust, which also have their effects on loyalty. A personalized relationship, built on communication, is more trusting and more satisfactory – in short, a "closer" relationship – and more likely to endure. Personalization adds psychological comfort to relationships and increases the psychological barriers to switching. Personalization increases benevolence trust, which is built up over time; therefore, switching service providers becomes a risk. Furthermore, personalization increases satisfaction, and switching providers may now involve an increased risk of lower satisfaction. So, for all these psychological dynamics, personalization of services is a substantial cause of loyalty.
>
> (Ball et al., 2006, 398)

Similarly, Mittal and Lassar (1996) investigated the impact of personalization in retail settings. Their findings further support the notion that "… for a business delivering service in interactive encounters with customers, 'personalization' emerges as the most important determinant of perceived service quality, and customer satisfaction and other patronage indicators" (Mittal & Lassar, 1996, 95). In a similar context, this was also supported in a study by Srinivasan et al. (2002). Finally, in a banking setting, Tong et al. (2014) found that service personalization has a significant positive impact on customer satisfaction and e-loyalty.

Why does personalization work? In one of the very few studies to provide data-driven insights into this, Bock et al. (2016) investigated the emotional and cognitive mechanisms driving the effects of personalization. They surveyed over 500 participants to understand how service personalization makes customers think and feel and to what it leads. First, they found that personalization indeed leads to higher loyalty, reconfirming the findings of other scholars we discussed. However, what is more interesting is what drives loyalty. Bock et al. discovered that the path from personalization to loyalty consists of two steps. Step 1: being offered personalization delights people and makes them experience gratitude. Step 2: delight and gratitude increase trust in the frontline employee, which, Step 3: increases attitudinal (or stated) loyalty toward the company. In short, if you offer personalization, customers will be delighted and will experience gratitude for what you did, which will make them trust you more, leading to higher loyalty.

Before concluding this subchapter, it is important to note that while digital businesses seem like the natural domain for personalization, companies offering tangible products are not excluded. The reason is two-fold. On the one hand, with the latest developments in production technology, companies can allow customers to customize products themselves and manufacture them with the same efficiency as mass products.

Perhaps the bigger reason personalization is not solely the domain of digital businesses but of all is that the term can mean two interrelated yet different things. The first is probably the more intuitive one, and it concerns the customization of the offering itself. This includes all the cases in which a company personalizes the product or the service. Some businesses are inherently personalized, and these can be found across domains as diverse as hairdressers and business consultants. While they would have certain solutions or methodologies, they would ultimately deliver a personalized product.

The second way that products or services can be personalized is to customize the service process, and this is the way we predominantly use the term in proactive personalized post-sales service (PPPS). Our focus is on what happens after the sales are made, i.e., on the value-creation stage of the process. Almost naturally, the customization of the offering is out of the question, as it had already been delivered. There is simply no opportunity for the company to customize its product or service at this point.

What any company can do, though, is to personalize its post-sales service to help customers create more value with its product or service. All of the things we discussed before and will see done in practice in the coming chapters can be personalized. From inspiration, through motivation, to education and making adjustments on the fly, you can take actions to personalize the experience and make it relevant for a specific customer at a specific point in time and deliver it in the right manner. It is a well-known leadership approach to apply different strategies to motivate the different members of your team. If you strive to do this for your team, why not do it for your customers?

Assuming that you are inspired and motivated by what you read so far, we now move to a discussion of the third requirement to doing post-sales service brilliantly – doing it at scale. A formidable challenge if there ever was one.

Proactive, Personalized Post-Sales Service at Scale

The first two requirements for a successful post-sales program – proactive and personalized – are not too difficult to meet in some businesses. Take a small B2B consulting business, like the one I have the pleasure to lead, as an example. We have approximately 15 key accounts and a wider list, including about 20 more. Within these 35 companies, we probably have around 100 key stakeholders. That is, there are about 100 people upon which the vast majority of our business depends. This is a really small number. We currently have a team of about ten account managers, which means that each takes care of about ten key stakeholders. Clearly, even if you wanted, you can't interact with all of them every day, so managing a group of stakeholders of this size is not even a full-time job. This allows our account managers to go the extra mile and search for ways to be proactive. For example, they keep our customers informed of the latest developments within the company by sending them personal emails (not newsletters – customized emails). They also proactively arrange quarterly business review sessions and try to drive the agenda. Needless to say, there are topics that our customers want to talk to us about in these meetings, and we are only happy to oblige, but we also ensure to include topics that will help our customers create more value out of our services. And, of course, what we try to do is anticipate what our stakeholders would need tomorrow or a week or a month from now. We don't have a high enough customer base to run data analytics, but our experience and listening to what customers are saying rarely mislead us.

Now, this process works for us, but then again, I'm talking about 100 people. Things become much more difficult if you have a thousand or a million customers. Like any other advancement from smaller to bigger scale, the solution is to automate the post-sales (value-creation) process.

There are two particular challenges that a company of this size will face when trying to automate the post-sales service to offer it at scale. The first one is a knowledge challenge and has to do with having a good idea of what to embed in the automation itself. For example, if you don't know what's the best course of action immediately after the customer has bought the product, or if you don't know that they just bought the product in the first place, that is a knowledge problem. You simply don't know that you need to act or what to do. The second challenge is automating the actions. Once you know that now is the right time to engage with the customer and you know how to do it, the question becomes one of implementing these actions.

I'd like to propose that the first question – do you know what to do? – is the one companies are less well-equipped to answer. The implementation question has been solved in a variety of domains for decades. Broadly, it involves either productizing as much as possible the service element or making the most of the latest technologies to automate actions.

It might seem odd to use the term productization to services, but this is the equivalent of manufacturing products at scale, only here we are manufacturing service delivery. The key is to remove as much as possible the personal element and unify frontline employees' appearance and behavior and the process they follow. It is not without a reason that contact centers resemble factories, and customers interactions happen in a conveyor-belt style. A customer calls (steps on the belt); the service rep introduces themself and asks how they can help. After the customer explains the question, the service rep follows the standard procedure for solving the issue or answering the question. There are no digressions or emotions, just a clear cold-headed interaction. After all, success in service centers is more often than not measured in resolution times. It is speed and efficiency that they are after, not delight.

The second way to solve the action implementation challenge isn't by seeing people-as-technology, but by using technology. Marketing automation platforms have been with us for quite some time, and the market is expected to reach almost USD 14.2 billion by 2030, with a compound annual growth rate (CAGR) of 12.3% (PR Newswire 2021). With the functionalities provided by most major players, automating the actions a company would like to take is made easy.

When it comes to actions, achieving scale is an easy feat. What is less so is knowing how to provide post-sales service in a proactive and personalized fashion at scale and what actions to take for a specific customer at a particular point in time. This is also reflected in the widely shared uncertainty among CX leaders about the return on investment (ROI) of the programs they run. According to a McKinsey survey, only 4% of leaders are confident that their measurement system allows them to calculate the impact of their actions (McKinsey & Company, 2021a).

The issue is rooted mainly in data creation and availability. There is a lot of talk, and I've heard from many of my clients that they have enough data and what they need is actions. That might very well be so; indeed, many companies run extensive research programs, collect user-generated content from social media, analyze the complaints they receive, and so on. Yet, two questions immediately come up when we start talking about using this data. Is that data the right data? And, somewhat paradoxically, do you have access to the data?

We will talk about these in a later chapter, but it's worth making some initial observations here. The right data, I believe, that will enable a truly proactive and personalized post-sales program at scale is connected data that you can tap on any time you need. The volume of data is not an issue; data can be created fairly quickly and easily. The challenge is connecting the dots for every customer, which typically takes the form of behavioral, transactional, and survey data. Such a data lake would allow for an innumerable amount of analytics – from the traditional descriptive analytics, through diagnostic, to predictive and prescriptive ones. The latter two are what companies that are serious about proactively addressing customer needs would need to engage. For that, they would need to have a constantly and seamlessly updated data lake of customer data. Again, as I have seen it, the challenge is not with data availability; this data very often does reside somewhere in the organization or at the very least can be created. Rather, the challenge is with crossing and connecting organizational siloes.

PPPS in Practice

I hope that everything we discussed so far gives a clear outline of what I believe will be the future for customer-centric companies. If the logic of our observations holds, in the coming years, businesses will start paying more attention to the post-sales service process, which is the phase at which the customer actually creates value with their products and services. They can do a lot to help customers maximize this value – they can inspire, motivate, and educate them, and they can offer adjustments in their delivery on the fly. The best-in-class post-sales programs will be done in a proactive and personalized fashion, and companies will be able to execute on these at scale. For example, they will no longer wait for customers to flag an issue to address it but would anticipate the issue and address it before it happens. Companies will also do this in a personalized fashion; specific customers have specific needs and questions at specific times, and organizations will find ways to address them in exactly this way. Finally, the leaders in post-sales service will run their programs at scale. They would be able to proactively address the specific needs of, potentially, all their customers.

This future is in fact already here, "it's just not evenly distributed", as the memorable phrase of William Gibson goes. It is high time that we discuss some excellent examples of companies already providing PPPS. This is where we turn to next.

Adobe

Adobe offers a great case study with its Lightroom product. Adobe Lightroom is one of the most popular products for photographic image storage, organization, and editing. Like many other things, photography can be quite difficult to learn, for there is a host of elements one needs to do well. Taking the image aside, processing it can be a significant hurdle as one needs to adjust a myriad of things that should also look well combined. From exposure and contrast, through white balance and highlights, to more sophisticated adjustments in the hue of specific colors, adding texture, or working with gradients, a photographer has many ways to edit their image to achieve the desired effect.

The early versions of Adobe Lightroom, like many other products, didn't include any Customer Education – one had to either experiment or learn from others. At one point, Adobe added a learning center in Lightroom, which meant that anyone willing to learn didn't have to leave the platform anymore – all the resources one needed were there.

The latest version of Adobe Lightroom brings this one step further to implementing the proactive, personalized post-sales paradigm. In October 2021, Adobe introduced a feature that "automatically recommends presets to you based on your photo" (Adobe, Feature summary | Lightroom; October 2021 release) The software creates a curated list of "Recommended Presets … inspired by edits made by users in the Lightroom in-app community. Lightroom compares photos with similar histograms and subjects to customize the preset options for you" (Adobe, Feature summary | Lightroom; October 2021 release). In other words, Adobe Lightroom is now offering extended post-sales service in the form of education. It is proactive in that Adobe provides it instead of waiting for customers to ask for it; it is personalized because it is based on the customer's specific photograph. Voila, proactive, personalized post-sales service.

Garmin

In a completely different industry, Garmin is another company that offers PPPS to its customers. Among its other product, Garmin manufactures one of the most popular GPS sports watches, typically used by its customers to track day-to-day health indicators like heart rate and sleep quality, and sports activities like running, swimming, cycling, and many others.

Garmin could stop there as it already offers so much data. But it goes one step further – it offers insights based on your activities. These are rather simple snippets like you are walking more than other users or sleeping less than them. What is more, Garmin offers customers ideas for improving their sleep or decreasing the amount of stress they are experiencing. Lastly, Garmin also offers personalized training plans. Customers can now select their goal, provide a couple of things Garmin needs to consider (like how often they train), and get a personalized plan for reaching their goal. Post-sales as in keeping the engagement after the sales are made – check. Proactive as in giving it to customers without having them ask for it – check. Personalized as in based on their specific situation – check.

Amazon

Amazon is a company that is frequently used as an example. Whether it's because of its customer service or in a more negative aspect, as a 'killer' of smaller businesses. Controversies like the latter aside, there's a lot I believe we can learn from the way they do business. What impressed me strongly recently is this story told by the blogger Chris Meadows. He and a friend became accustomed to watching movies online together on rabb.it – an app that allows you to "play video streams from nearly any web-accessible video service—YouTube, Netflix, Hulu, Amazon, etc" (Meadows, 2018). As

Meadows tells the story, the problem is that the app sometimes cuts out, so you need to refresh the page. So far, a typical story.

What I find amazing is how Amazon dealt with this. Meadows gives the full text of the email he received from them, and it's an example of how to do PPPS. Check it out:

Hello,

We noticed that you recently experienced poor video playback on Amazon Video. We're sorry for the inconvenience and have issued you a refund for the following rental(s) and amount(s):

$2.99 – The Big Sleep (1946), Season null the Big Sleep (1946)

While Amazon Video transactions are typically not refundable, we are happy to make an exception in this case. This refund should be processed within the next 2 to 3 business days and will appear on your next billing statement for the same credit card used to purchase this item.

Please visit our troubleshooting page for tips on ways you can potentially improve your viewing experience.

We hope to see you again soon,
Amazon Video Team

(Meadows, 2018)

Proactive? Check! Personalized? Check (they quote the exact movie they are refunding for)! Post-sales? Clearly. Could Amazon just leave things without making any effort? Of course. But they didn't, and that made an impression on the customer. In Chris' words,

… by being proactive and refunding it without being asked, Amazon creates or reinforces the impression that it cares about my experience, making me all the more likely to purchase from Amazon in the future, and more likely to tell my friends I had a surprisingly good experience with the business rather than an annoyingly crummy one. All that potential extra loyalty, for just three bucks.

(Meadows, 2018)

I can't say it better than this.

Further Ideas

Once you start thinking about post-sales service as the time when value is created, many ideas come to you. For example, taxi companies know a lot about their customers. Can they offer a ride back if they see that the outbound address is a destination from which people often get a cab? Or if they have regular customers who take a cab every day from the same location to go to work or somewhere else – can they proactively schedule a car for them?

Supermarkets and grocery stores can also do a much better job at this. They send promotional materials over email, yet I don't see them personalized. Come to think about it, with loyalty programs and online shopping on the rise, they know so much about the products I consume. Can supermarkets tailor their offers a bit better? It could be that I don't care about this beef that they have on offer this week, but I might consider buying eggs. I bet you that this is predictable by online stores' purchase data. And what makes this substantially different from simple cross-selling is the fact that I actually care about, say, eggs.

The same goes for hairdressers, for example. Reminders about scheduling an appointment can be an excellent way to drive more reoccurring business. What's more, they can also share tips and tricks for managing my new hairstyle in the weeks after I get it. Is it wet today? Well, here's an opportunity for my hairdresser to give me some advice. Windy? No problem, they've got me covered.

By extension, shoe sellers can do the same. I really don't want to receive ideas for the best ways to keep my shoes looking good on a normal day. But I might be interested in such advice the day it starts snowing, or even the week before. Oh, and I care for the shoes I have in particular, not about this model that is the most popular one.

What PPPS Is Not

Before we conclude this chapter, we need to make one very important point – post-sales service is not cross-selling and up-selling. While it may result in the purchase of more products or services from the company, this is not the goal. Simply because the focus is not on 'How can we sell more?' but on 'How can we help more (and in the process sell more)?' Really caring for customers means that sometimes the company might even act, on the surface, against its interests. For example, can Netflix[2] suggest that I have a break and have a walk in the park instead of suggesting another movie to watch after I've watched a movie? Or can it offer a deeper experience to some interested customers by suggesting that I read a book related to a movie I've watched? This, I believe, is what caring about customers is about, not nudging them to binge-watch endlessly.

Neither are simple newsletters post-sales service, especially in the form they usually take. Broadcasting news about your company might have its benefits for you, and that's a completely valid thing to do. Yet, they tend to be long documents with articles written by company experts or marketeers that, in my opinion, rarely help create any value whatsoever. As we will see later, the major reason for this is that they are completely impersonalized and address mostly generic topics of common interest. In this format, they are fundamentally unfit to help customers create value simply because they address questions very few people have when receiving the newsletter.

The list of things companies do that mostly serve them can continue. Again, I'm not saying that you should stop doing them – that would be a terrible combination of ignorance and arrogance on my end. Newsletters and cross-selling campaigns and all the other things companies do to become or remain at the top of customers' minds or nudge them to do something have their very valid place in the toolbox or marketeers. But they are not enough to truly help customers create value.

Chapter Summary

In the first chapter, we identified post-sales service of the customer journey as the critical point at which companies can and should stay close to their customers to help them create more value with their products or services. As discussed, companies can do this broadly via four different initiatives: they can inspire, motivate, educate customers, and make adjustments in the delivery of their products and services on the fly.

In this chapter, we built on this framework and looked at the elements that would make a post-sales program truly customer-centric and future-proof. We described the world-class post-sales program as one that allows companies to be proactive in the interaction, offer personalization, and do this at scale. We saw what benefits companies can expect from such a program. We closed by going through a handful of examples of companies already providing PPPS and tried to demonstrate the kind of thinking PPPS unlocks by applying the framework to others.

In the next chapter, we will look at what's stopping companies from doing PPPS today, and more specifically – where are the current solutions they use failing them.

Notes

1 See also Hutchinson and Barrett (2019).
2 I need to make an important point here: I both like and admire Netflix for what they have accomplished. This example is merely to make a point and in no way suggests that Netflix is providing bad customer experience.

References

Adobe. (October 2021 release). Feature summary | Lightroom. Retrieved from https://helpx.adobe.com/lightroom-cc/using/whats-new/2022.html#reco mmended_presets

Ball, D., Coelho, P. S., & Vilares, M. J. (2006). Service personalization and loyalty. *Journal of Services Marketing*, 20(6), 391–403. doi:10.1108/08876040610691284

Barrett, L. F. (2020). *Seven and a half lessons about the brain*. Kindle Edition. HMH Books. New York.

Becker, J. U., Spann, M., & Barrot, C. (2020). Impact of Proactive Postsales Service and Cross-Selling Activities on Customer Churn and Service Calls. *Journal of Service Research*, 23(1), 53–69. https://doi.org/10.1177/1094670519883347

Bock, D. E., Mangus, S. M., & Folse, J. A. G. (2016). The road to customer loyalty paved with service customization. *Journal of Business Research*, 69(10), 3923–3932. doi:10.1016/j.jbusres.2016.06.002

Clark, A. (2013). Whatever next? Predictive brains, situated agents, and the future of cognitive science. *Behavioral and Brain Sciences*, 36(3), 181–204. doi:10.1017/S0140525X12000477

de Lange, F. P., Heilbron, M., & Kok, P. (2018, September). How do expectations shape perception? *Trends in Cognitive Sciences*, 22(9), 764–779. doi:10.1016/j.tics.2018.06.002. PMID: 30122170

Hutchinson, J. B., & Barrett, L. F. (2019). The power of predictions: An emerging paradigm for psychological research. *Current Directions in Psychological Science*, 28(3), 280–291. doi:10.1177/0963721419831992

McKinsey & Company. (2021a). Prediction: The future of CX. Retrieved from www.mckinsey.com/business-functions/marketing-and-sales/our-insights/prediction-the-future-of-cx

McKinsey & Company. (2021b). The value of getting personalization right—Or wrong—Is multiplying. Retrieved from www.mckinsey.com/business-functions/marketing-and-sales/our-insights/the-value-of-getting-personalization-right-or-wrong-is-multiplying

Meadows, C. (2018). An unexpected Amazon refund demonstrates just how clever Jeff Bezos can be. Retrieved from https://teleread.org/2018/05/06/an-unexpected-amazon-refund-demonstrates-just-how-clever-jeff-bezos-can-be/

Mittal, B., & Lassar, W. M. (1996). The role of personalization in service encounters. *Journal of Retailing*, 72(1), 95–109. doi:10.1016/S0022-4359(96)90007-X

Retana, G. F., Forman, C., & Wu, D. J. (2015, April 26). Proactive customer education, customer retention, and demand for technology support: Evidence from a field experiment. Manufacturing and Service Operations Management. Available at SSRN. Retrieved from https://ssrn.com/abstract=2430012 or http://dx.doi.org/10.2139/ssrn.2430012

Shin, H., Ellinger, A.E., Mothersbaugh, D.L. & Reynolds, K.E. (2017), Employing proactive interaction for service failure prevention to improve customer service experiences. *Journal of Service Theory and Practice, 27(1)*, 164-186. https://doi.org/10.1108/JSTP-07-2015-0161

Srinivasan, S. S., Anderson, R. E., & Ponnavolu, K. (2002). Customer loyalty in e-commerce: An exploration of its antecedents and consequences. *Journal of Retailing*, 78(1), 41–50. doi:10.1016/S0022-4359(01)00065-3

Tong, C., Wong, S. K-S., & Lui, K. P-H. (2014). The influences of service personalization, customer satisfaction and switching costs on E-loyalty. doi:10.5539/ijef.v4n3p105

Voorhees, C. M., Brady, M. K., & Horowitz, D. M. (2006, October). A voice from the silent masses: An exploratory and comparative analysis of noncomplainers. *Journal of the Academy of Marketing Science*, 34(4), 514–527. doi:10.1177/0092070306288762

3 The Limitations of the Existing Post-Sales Service Initiatives

Everything we discussed so far is not to say that companies completely ignore post-sales services (the value-creation phase of the journey). I know of a myriad of organizations throughout the whole world, big and small, that are trying to get to the vision we outlined – doing post-sales service in a proactive, personalized, and scalable fashion, and importantly – to help their customers create more value for themselves and benefit from the process. Yet, examples like the ones we saw from Adobe, Garmin, and Liberty Global are still rare.

I'm not a huge fan of using anecdotal evidence, but the above observation got me to dig deeper into my own experiences. I found that virtually none of the companies I buy products or services from, apart from Garmin and Adobe, had offered me proactive, personalized post-sales service. True, some of them asked for my feedback which I duly shared. But if I need to initiate the conversation, it's not really a company-initiated action, is it?

I use two different companies for online shopping for groceries. They are both great; I like the variety and prices. Both companies call me to ask for my feedback after every purchase. Yet, I have never received from them neither an inspiration, nor motivation, nor education on how to actually use the products I buy. There are tons of things they can do. For example, they can motivate me to cook more by showing me my impact on the environment when I cook at home vs. when I order food for home vs. when I eat out. Or they can send me recipes that include the products I bought from them. Or they can send me promotions for products I bought from them the last time.

Literally, as I was finishing the last paragraph, I received an email with promotions from the company from which I used to order food online. It was one of these emails that made me ask, political correctness aside, "What is wrong with you people?" I have never ordered food from McDonald's. I have not been in any of their brick-and-mortar places in ages. I frequently order from vegan and vegetarian places, and more broadly, I fancy hip places. Who decided that I might be interested in McDonald's? There is one logic that makes sense, but it goes contrary to helping me realize more value. One can potentially claim that I'm a good target to increase their trial base as I have never ordered from them. But that is a company-centric logic; what this does is leave me feeling like a number in their purchase funnel, which

DOI: 10.4324/9781003309284-5

I'm sure I am. Ranting aside, this episode didn't have any positive result for them and frustrated me because it distracted me from what I was doing.

Moving on to my multicooker. I have used it exactly three times in the last two years (not much of a cook, I know). Could I use it more? Sure, but (a) I need to be reminded about it, (b) I need to be motivated to do it ("food is much healthier when steam-cooked", for example), and (c) I need education; I need them to show me, step-by-step, what to do.

Or take the place where I print photographs; I print probably 20–30 small photos per week, using the same printing center. The other day they sent me their generic newsletter to tell me that they are offering a discount on larger prints. That could count as proactive, but it can't count as personalized. Because I send them my photos online, they actually have a rather large archive of photos taken by me. Is it difficult, I wonder, instead of using a generic image in the promotional email, to show me how good my photos would look printed on a bigger scale? Or can they, for example, help me by telling me that next time I'd better use this other paper for my photos because they will look better?

And one final example – this time from an online sports goods retailer. Running shoes typically last about 500 km before you need to change them (that's what the manufacturers say). However, many people wear them much longer (me included). It is also true that the online retailer doesn't know how much running I do per month. Yet, they can get it right with a couple of reasonable assumptions and trial-and-error. I have never received an email from any of the two places I shop for running shoes saying:

> Hey Ivaylo! A couple of months ago you bought [this and that brand of running shoes from us]. We know that they typically last about 500km, so we wanted to check if it's time for you to change them. We have the same model in our shop, and it's discounted. Would you like us to ship it to you?

I guarantee that I would buy at least one extra pair per year with this approach.

All of this isn't meant as a critique for these companies. I wanted to merely point out the vast opportunities companies miss when they disengage from me after the sales are made. And I think they do this because of their underappreciation for the actual value-creation process. Even with the best of their intentions, the existing solutions cannot bring them to offer proactive, personalized post-sales service.

Adjustments on the Fly: Complaint Management

Perhaps the oldest and clearly one of the most effective solutions for delivering post-sales service is traditional complaint management. Its basic flow of operation is this: the company provides a way for the customer to contact it to report an issue -> the customer contacts the company -> the company offers a satisfactory solution. It includes, for example, management of formal complaints, providing product returns, and offering product repair and/or maintenance. There is rarely a company in the world these days that doesn't do that, to a bigger or smaller extend; this is also driven by government regulations for customer protection, a lot of which require companies to allow customers to return products for free within a certain period, for example.

Why Is it a Good Idea to Allow or Even Encourage Customers to Complain?

Although most companies do complaint management, few would encourage customers to complain. This seems like an odd thing to say, but it's often better to have customers talk to you than to others. A low or decreasing number of complaints might mean that customers have nothing to complain about; yet, it could also mean that customers just don't complain and leave the company instead.

Studies show that customers who complain are twice less likely to spread negative word-of-mouth. Nyer and Gopinath (2005), for example, discovered that allowing customers to vent their dissatisfaction is enough to decrease their urge to tell others about it, thus doing much less harm to the business – only 16% of the complaining customers spread negative word-of-mouth. In comparison, 37% of the non-complaining customers spoke negatively about the brand with others. In addition, it is only among the group of people who complained that satisfaction increased considerably in time. Satisfaction of customers who neither spread negative word-of-mouth nor complained increased marginally in the period they studied; satisfaction of customers who complained also increased, interestingly, albeit also marginally. Among those who complained, satisfaction increased by 0.7 points on a 7-pt scale, which is about six times higher than the increase in the other two groups. By telling others about their experience, the latter group became committed to their view, cemented their dissatisfaction.

The latter finding that satisfaction level among customers who complain could be higher than before their issue is known as the service recovery paradox. It is also aptly demonstrated in the study by Voorhees et al, which we discussed in a previous chapter. As a reminder, repeat purchase intention in their study was higher and negative word-of-mouth was lower among customers who complained and received a satisfactory recovery than those who never complained.

These insights show that good complaint management is a must for any company that wants to help its customers create value, and it benefits the company hugely. In fact, companies might be better off encouraging or at the very least making it easier for customers to complain. After all, if a customer is unhappy, you'd better know about it and act to mitigate the damage rather than pretend that there isn't a problem at all, right?

Why You Can't Rely on Customer Complaint Management to Do PPPS

No matter how easy you make it for customers to complain though, you will eventually face three limitations of using complaint management alone to provide post-sales service.

Complaint management is an inherently defensive game – you are waiting for customers to tell you that something is wrong before you can make adjustments. This makes it a reactive solution; if something wrong happens, you will act, but first, you need to know that something wrong has happened. Proactive post-sales service is far out of reach for complaint management practices.

Second, complaint management cannot do anything to inspire and motivate customers. Support lines do offer education, of course – after all, doing this is why they are called 'support' lines in the first place. But the very nature of how the interaction is initiated almost precludes the service agent from offering inspiration or motivation. In most cases, they would limit themselves to answering the caller's question, and that's only normal given the likely frustration on the customer's end.

The second reason why complaint management cannot help you deliver proactive, personalized post-sales service is that it lacks scalability and is a reactive practice. Over 50 years ago, Albert Hirschman showed that people generally have three choices when dealing with organizations: exit, voice, and loyalty. They can be unhappy and leave; they can be unhappy and raise their concerns; or they can be happy and stay. The thing is, much more customers prefer Exit over Voice; especially when it's easy to switch companies, customers would rather do that than complain. As John Goodman puts it in Customer Experience 3.0, when talking about customer complaints "No news is not necessarily good news"; "Companies are not aware of the number of customers who are dissatisfied because relatively few customers with problems complain. Instead of complaining, most people become less loyal and spread negative word-of-mouth" (Goodman, 2014, 21).

In other words, every company will face what is known as the customer complaint iceberg. This is a fancy name for a simple phenomenon – not every unhappy customer will complain. Just how big is this iceberg? Some authors like Adrian Swinscoe (2010) estimate it to be about 4%, i.e., only 1 in 25 unhappy customers will log in a complaint. Going further, he suggests that for every customer complaint that you receive, unhappy customers will spread word-of-mouth, reaching 1,300 other people. He bases both of his estimates on a study conducted by the US company TARP in 1999. Other sources put the tip of the iceberg at about 6% (Knowledge@Wharton, 2006).

However, the number of unhappy customers who complain is likely quite low, although it probably varies with the size of the purchase and the severity of the problem. Either way, I think we can accept with certainty that we are far off the 100% mark, which leaves us many unhappy customers on the loose.

Given all of this, it is no wonder that companies are looking for ways to gain the same benefits but on a bigger scale. A solution that increases the scale at which companies can address customer dissatisfaction does exist, albeit only a partial one – it is known as close-the-loop programs.

Adjustments on the Fly: Close-the-Loop Initiatives

As the name implies, close-the-loop programs are about going a full circle. In the case of customer experience, it is a circle that starts with customer feedback, goes through the company taking action, and goes back to the customer. As you can see, its basic workflow is not substantially different from that of complaint management programs. The major difference between the two is who initiates this loop. In the case of complaint management, the customer has the leading role. In the case of close-the-loop programs, the company initiates the dialogue. This is indeed a major advancement from simply waiting for customers to tell you things. With close-the-loop, you are actively engaging customers in a conversation, so in our terms, it is a solution that allows you to be more proactive in complaint management.

Close-the-loop programs have become commonplace for companies that want to improve customer experience. At the time I am writing this, the customer experience management market is booming. In 2020, it was estimated to be about USD 7.5 billion, "and is expected to grow at a CAGR of 17.5% from 2021 to 2028" (Grand View Research, 2021). Clearly, this also includes other market segments. However, it still paints a clear enough picture – close-the-loop programs and the software and analytics accompanying and unlocking them are here to stay.

There is a very good reason for that. Close-the-loop programs work and can substantially improve customer experience and bring financial benefits to the company. As a case in point, look at the evolution of the close-the-loop program of Signify, the world leader in lighting for professionals, consumers, and the Internet of Things.

As light is a prerequisite for all human activity, the customer ecosystem of Signify is complex. It ranges from home-users to business users, from retailers, architects and designers, to installers, turning these requirements into reality. Being the leader in lighting and at the forefront of innovation, Signify offers solutions ranging from traditional light bulbs and luminaires, through LED products, to connected lighting systems and services. For years, they have run a successful close-the-loop program based on Net Promoter Score (NPS), which was also part of the incentive scheme of key roles within the company. The program was executed by conducting telephone interviews with customers twice a year, reporting the results in PowerPoint and Excel, and customer experience specialists following up on the customer feedback.

In early 2019, Signify realized that to remain relevant to customers and keep advancing their close-the-loop program, they had to change the way it worked. On the one hand, running the survey twice a year was far from enough in the dynamic business environment in which they operate. By the time they took action, often detractors had already left the company. In addition, the lack of a system allowing for seamless execution of the survey and quick decision-making made the process slow and cumbersome, resulting in limited employee engagement with the program instead of them taking ownership to improve customer experience.

This all changed when Signify implemented a digital solution for collecting and analyzing customer feedback, with an embedded action manager that allows them to take action quickly and, importantly, increases the program's visibility. Now, they run their overall relationship study every quarter and supplement it with surveys around specific transactions and other event-triggered surveys. This shift to a digital solution allowed them, in 2019 alone, to reach 20% more customers on 30% more markets and act more and faster, all within the same budget. In addition, while previously it took them weeks to take action, now 80% of all unhappy customers are contacted by Signify within 72 hours from leaving the feedback. Further, every two weeks, they review the common issues encountered by customers to take higher-level actions to tackle them. This setup allows Signify to take over 250 market-related customer experience initiatives per quarter. The results are impressive. As a result of this transformation of their program and increased focus on improvement actions management, Signify has been witnessing three consecutive quarters of steady NPS growth since Q3 2019. By Q2 2020, NPS had increased by 10 points.

A second brilliant example of how running a good close-the-loop program can benefit customers and companies alike comes from HeidelbergCement Group, a leading building materials manufacturer. One typically wouldn't expect it from a company in this industry. Yet, they have implemented one of the most impressive customer experience programs I have seen, part of which is a close-the-loop program. As Judith van Herwaarden, Global Principal – Customer Experience at the company, explains,

> More than 10 years ago, HeidelbergCement Group set out on a transformational journey to achieve operational excellence on all of its markets. The decision was driven by the strive for continuous improvement, embedded in the organization's DNA, its deep-rooted engineering legacy, and other strengths. The transformation propelled HeidelbergCement Group to a global leadership position in their industry, but, driven by the exponential changes in the business environment, the company's executives had to take a new transformational direction to maintain leadership.[1]

A particularly important challenge that their whole industry faced was the lack of differentiation between the players, which created the conditions for a price war threatening to undermine the company's position. With this in mind, the company created a customer-centric culture to better understand customer needs, which allowed them to offer exceptional customer experience, a point of differentiation, and a solid foundation for sustainable growth.

Early in the process, HeidelbergCement Group implemented a digital solution to collect, analyze, and act on customers' feedback. The technological solution was complemented by a tremendous effort by their Customer Experience team, which organized hundreds of workshops around the globe to drive engagement within the program. As of 2021, the close-the-loop program of HeidelbergCement Group is rolled out to 43 markets. In 2019, they closed the loop with 80% of the customers who shared feedback via the surveys they run; this amounts to approximately 3,000 customer engagements in 2019 as part of the close-the-loop program alone. In addition, due to the efforts to promote a customer-centric culture, the company's employees have realized over 2,100 improvement initiatives.

The results from the program justify the investment. Like Signify, HeidelbergCement Group is seeing a substantial uplift in NPS, with the accompanying benefits. Van Herwaarden continues,

> Repeated studies have shown that Promoters, the most loyal customers, have a higher customer lifetime value by spending 19% more with HeidelbergCement Group and being less price sensitive. One of those showed that on average, promoters spend 22% more with the company than detractors, and have accepted 3% higher price increases than detractors. And, especially in developing markets, there is a visible shift from commodity and volume-price selling to strategic partnerships and value-based relations with customers".[2]

What both of these examples show, in short, is that close-the-loop programs can do an incredibly good job in improving customer experience and bring benefits to the company doing it – a fantastic example of a win–win situation. Nevertheless, close-the-loop programs suffer from the same inherent limitations as complaint management. Although proactive in searching for feedback and initiating an interaction with the customer, they are still not fully proactive in addressing customer needs as they rely on clients to reply to a survey. What is more, although they increase the reach of post-sales service programs by expanding the pool of people covered compared to complaint management alone, they are still far from giving a view over the entire customer base. After the customer complaint iceberg, we can call the latter challenge the survey response iceberg.

There is no official data related to survey response rates, but the estimates of different companies provide a good start. In a limited meta-analytic exercise, Survey Anyplace puts the survey response rate at an average of 33%, with email and online surveys slightly lower (30% and 29%, respectively) (Survey Anyplace, 2021). PeoplePulse, based on their experience in the US, puts the average response rate for online surveys at 41% (PeoplePulse). Pew Research Center (Pew Research Center, 2017) reported response rates for telephone surveys in the US to be 9% in 2016. And last, CustomerThermometer claims that "Survey response rates in the 5% to 30% range are far more typical" (CustomerThermometer). In my experience, while broad, the latter estimation is quite accurate. It is indeed a rare occurrence to see response rates of over 30%, and they can go much lower, depending on the survey specifics, of course.

Whichever estimate is the correct one, we are still far off the 100% coverage of the customer base mark. This issue is further exaggerated because we are talking about continuous monitoring of customer satisfaction (or NPS, or any other metric). If you can reach a third of your customer base in a single survey, that's excellent news! The problem is, can you do this every month? And if not, what's to guarantee that a customer that is happy today won't turn into a detractor next month?

Initiatives for Customer Inspiration, Motivation, and Education

In the first chapter of the book, we outlined a view of marketing that underscores that the value customers derive from products and services is always at least partially co-created by them. In light of this, we propose that from a company perspective, post-sales service is critical for supporting customers in this, and we broadly lumped the initiatives they can initiate into two groups – customer inspiration, motivation, education, and adjustments on the fly. So far in this chapter, we discussed with specific examples how companies are currently doing the latter and the potential drawbacks of the existing solutions.

In the remainder of the chapter, we will look at what companies can do to inspire, motivate, and educate customers. There is no shortage of solutions for this. Product manuals explaining the basic operations of the product, for example, fall into this category. So do frequently asked questions companies put on their websites; they also count as a self-service element. The forums companies maintain that allow user-to-user interaction are another way to offer inspiration, motivation, and education to customers. In these, more knowledgeable, one hopes, customers often share their advice on how others can do certain things with the product or service provided by the company.

The list can go on and on. Here are a couple of ideas from Skilljar, a company built "to be the best Customer Education platform in the world" (Skilljar):

- Recorded webinars: Great for providing a walk-through of a product's interface or when it would be helpful to have a human explain a complex topic.
- Recorded screen-captures: Ideal for sharing step-by-step instructions for complex configurations or processes.
- Infographics (PDF): These are opportunities to recycle existing marketing content for high-level overviews or fast facts.

- Slideshows: Another great way to repurpose content – in this case, consider uploading content that was previously used during in-person training.
- Quizzes & knowledge checks: These help students measure their level of understanding and can be a great way to keep them engaged with learning content.

Now, I'm a data fan. Whenever I read or hear a statement, I ask myself, "How do we know this?" and if there's limited empirical basis behind it, I tend to disregard it. That is why I hesitated for a long time before making the next observation, but as I found absolutely no data source to support or refute it, I'll give it a go. For some reason or another, a lot of companies shy away from inspiring, motivating, and most of all, educating their customers; software companies are a notable exception, and while it is true that by the nature of their business, it is easier for them to do this, it doesn't change the fact that it is a sound principle for all companies to follow. In my view, this happens because companies consider it as giving customers something pro-bono. What is probably worse, that once customers become savvier, they would switch to another supplier.

Educating customers makes them more loyal to the company. This was one of the findings reported by Bell and Eisingerich (2007), who investigated whether customer loyalty is related in any way to Customer Education in the financial industry. Working with a global investment services organization, they compiled

> A list of 4,244 clients, randomly generated from the population of 7,200 clients classified as "high value" by the firm. High-value clients were sampled due to the higher frequency of contact with advisors and the increased likelihood of respondents recalling and commenting on the quality of service they received. Data were collected via a self-administered questionnaire sent by mail to each respondent. The total number of usable responses was 1,268... .
>
> (Bell & Eisingerich, 2007, 473)

They asked these customers about their view of the interaction with the company in question, such as whether their advisor keeps them informed of the status of their investment, whether the advisor "explains financial concepts and recommendations in a meaningful way" (Bell & Eisingerich, 2007, 474), etc.

What Bell and Eisingerich discovered is that there is a direct relationship between Customer Education and customer loyalty, lending credence to the notion that helping customers create more value by teaching them the tricks of the trade is highly beneficial for the company. The authors explain:

> Clear explanations of financial concepts and the provision of essential information would be perceived as service augmentations by clients.

Client education is consistent with notions of relationship selling (Weitz and Bradford, 1999), where the sales process is more about partnership building with customers than the "hard sell" (Beverland, 2001). And the process is likely to be iterative, with customers "testing" their knowledge and assumptions about the management of their finances with their advisor – effectively seeking reassurance about their decisions (Harrison, 2002). This process will likely increase the bond between the client and the firm.

(Bell & Eisingerich, 2007, 478)

Similarly, Suh et al. (2015) conducted a survey in South Korea to investigate whether Customer Education increases loyalty. Like Bell and Eisingerich, they found out that it does. Moreover, they unraveled the path through which this happens. Customer Education increases trust in the organization. That is, the feeling "that the actions of the other party will bring positive outcomes" (Suh et al., 2015, 265). This higher trust then leads to higher evaluations by customers of service quality, which in turn makes them more loyal.

In addition, Adam Avramescu offers a host of other benefits companies can expect by educating their customers. These include, for example:

- "Customer Acquisition Cost: Customer Education can reduce the number of questions your Sales-humans answer repeatedly, and it can help you convert trials to paid plans effectively.
- Customer Lifetime Value (CLTV): The longer an account stays with you and the more they buy from you over time, the more value you derive. Customer Education helps to instill customer loyalty by building trust and accelerating value.
- Customer Maturity: Closely linked to CLTV is maturity, where customers can see the path to ongoing value over time. Many companies use maturity models to diagnose the customer's current state and set a path to a future state.
- Customer Sentiment or Loyalty: Typically measured with NPS, those 0–10 "Would you recommend this product?" surveys, customers are more likely to renew and expand over time if they're strong advocates of your product. Customer Education helps customers become loyal advocates by empowering them and connecting them with others.
- Product Adoption: The path to meaningful usage of a product is similar to how you would form any habit, like brushing your teeth. Customer Education helps users understand why they should do it and then build a habit around it.
- Brand Differentiation: If you are the "education leader" in your category, your brand will be seen as the expert. This makes buying decisions easier and also increases customer loyalty. It's much harder to win in your category without being able to prove that you know the space better than anyone else.

- Customer Self-Service Efficiency: Customers don't like calling for support. Helping users self-serve not only decreases your support costs, but it also decreases users' frustration" (Avramescu, 2019, 14-15).

If only part of this is as bright as these authors describe it, companies have every reason to invest more in Customer Education. What I would like to suggest, though, is that they do it in a proactive, personalized, and scalable fashion, and more importantly, to expand it beyond the immediate domain of your product or service.

Most of the Customer Education tools discussed above are suitable for delivering education at scale. But they are very rarely used in a personalized way, in the sense we discussed previously – delivering the answer when and where a customer needs it. Take webinars, for example; there is something everyone can take from any webinar. Yet, broadcasting a discussion on, say, building a successful close-the-loop program from scratch to someone who has been doing it for years is less than optimal. They simply need something more. Timing is of the essence here.

The best Customer Education programs, I believe, will deliver answers when the customers need them. What is more, they will do so proactively. This is not about blasting rewarmed content at customers, barely hiding a sales pitch under the disguise of Customer Education. Proactive education teaches customers what they can do more with your product or service. This would, I imagine, take the form of "Hey, customer! We see that you are doing A and B. You know what, you can also do C and D, just like this and that customer did! Here's how…". Timely? Check. Specific? Check! Addressing my need? Check. A little bit invasive? Also, check – we'll return to this point in the last chapter.

And finally, I believe one of the key functions of education is to expand horizons. Customer Education is no different. It is not so much about training customers to use your product. Customer Education is more about supporting them to create more value with it, which goes well beyond the scope of the immediate product or service offering. Going back to some of the examples we discussed before, the inspiration, motivation, and education Garmin offers are not so much about using their watch. It goes above and beyond and helps you live a better life. And in the fictional multicooker example, it's not about knowing which mode to use for cooking rice. It is about helping customers make a healthier or more delicious dinner.

These elements – proactiveness, personalization, going beyond the immediate scope of your value proposition – will be the key ingredients of customer inspiration, motivation, and education programs in the future and will bring considerable benefits to the companies doing them well.

Chapter Summary

While each of the initiatives we discussed in this chapter has its rightful place in a company's arsenal of post-sales activities, as we saw, each of them also comes with its limitations, summarized in Table 3.1. They are either reactive and lagging behind customer needs, not personalized, or not scalable, or a combination of these.

In making adjustments on the fly, managing customer complaints well has proven to be an indispensable part of what a company can do to help customers create more value with its products and services. There are, however, two issues inherent in this solution. On the one hand, not every unhappy customer will complain – far from it. The most widely accepted

Table 3.1 The Limitations of the Existing Post-Sales Initiatives

Initiative	Benefits	Allows for proactiveness?	Allows for personalization?	Allows for proactiveness and personalization at scale?
Complaint management	Practically, a must in today's business environment. Provides customers a way to flag potential value-destroying aspects of a product or service elements (flaws)	No, as it depends on customers flagging about value-destroying aspects	Personalization is inherent – every complaint is addressed separately	Cannot reach all customers potentially experiencing the same issue as not all customers will complain
Close-the-Loop programs	Substantially expand the scope of complaint management initiatives	Not fully, as companies are proactive in initiating an interaction with customers but cannot act without their feedback	Personalization is inherent – by definition the goal of close-the-loop programs is to address the feedback of specific customers	Expands the scope of complaint management initiatives but still cannot reach all customers as not all of them reply to surveys
Customer inspiration, motivation, and education initiatives, e.g., webinars, infographics, frequently asked questions	Provides significant business benefits to companies	Proactively provided by the company but usage is left at the discretion of the customer	Potentially yes but are rarely used in such a way	Potentially yes but are rarely used in such a way

estimations are that less than 10% of dissatisfied customers will contact the company to address it. This leaves many people who would potentially switch or spread negative word-of-mouth out in the open. In addition, complaint management is a defensive game in which a company reacts to customers complaining instead of leading the engagement. This puts the organization in a situation to deal with a customer who is very likely frustrated; it is fighting an uphill battle.

Close-the-loop programs come to the rescue to mitigate, if not completely erase, the downsides of complaint management. They are proactive in the sense that it is a company initiating the interaction, and they supplement complaint management to boost the scale at which a business engages with its customers. Yet, they don't fully solve the two challenges inherent in using complaint management to provide post-sales service. They still rely on customers sharing their feedback. Given that no company can interview all of its customers all the time, this still leaves a huge amount of potentially unhappy customers unaccounted for.

Finally, in the domain of customer inspiration, motivation, and education, companies who care about their customers offer them ways to self-educate by providing materials like product manuals, frequently asked questions, and tutorials. All of these initiatives surely work and increase the value customers can create with the company's products and services. Yet, as Adam and Dave Derington put it well,

> Customer Education is a function, a department, a practice — not just a series of ad hoc activities. You don't have a Customer Education function just because you run webinars or do training. You have a Customer Education function when you implement a strong core program based on sound Customer Education Strategy.
>
> (Customer.Education, 2020)

Moreover, you are educating customers when you personalize the approach to the needs of specific customers. This is the major inherent flaw in the initiatives listed at the beginning of this paragraph – they are simply not personalized enough, as anyone who has tried to find the answer to their very concrete question on a company's website can probably testify.

We can all do better than this. The proliferation of data and the availability of cutting-edge data analytics methods unlocks a huge opportunity for companies to change this and start offering proactive, personalized post-sales services. We will now discuss what companies can do to capitalize on this opportunity and present a roadmap for success.

Notes

1 Conversation with the author.
2 Conversation with the author.

References

Avramescu, A. (2019). *Customer education: Why smart companies profit by making customers smarter.* Kindle Edition.

Bell, S. J., & Eisingerich, A. B. (2007). The paradox of customer education: Customer expertise and loyalty in the financial services industry. *European Journal of Marketing,* 41(5/6), 466–486. doi:10.1108/03090560710737561

Customer.Education. (2020). Customer Education strategy: 6 principles for success. Retrieved from https://customer.education/2020/07/customer-education-6-principles/

CustomerThermometer. (2019). Average survey response rate—What you need to know. Retrieved from www.customerthermometer.com/customer-surveys/average-survey-response-rate/

Goodman, J. (2014). *Customer experience 3.0.* Kindle Edition. AMACOM, New York.

GrandView Research. (2021). Customer experience management market size, share and trends analysis report by end-use (BFSI, retail), by analytical tools. Retrieved from www.grandviewresearch.com/industry-analysis/customer-experience-management-market (pp. 2021–2028) (Speech, Text analytics), By Deployment (Cloud, On-premise), By Touch Point Type, and Segment Forecasts.

Knowledge@Wharton. (2006). Beware of dissatisfied consumers: They like to blab. Retrieved from https://knowledge.wharton.upenn.edu/article/beware-of-dissatisfied-consumers-they-like-to-blab/

Nyer, P. U., & Gopinath, M. (2005). Effects of complaining versus negative word of mouth on subsequent changes in satisfaction: The role of public commitment. *Psychology and Marketing,* 22(12), 937–953. doi:10.1002/mar.20092

PeoplePulse. Survey response rates. Tips on how to increase your survey response rates. Retrieved from https://peoplepulse.com/resources/useful-articles/survey-response-rates/

Pew Research Center. (2017). What low response rates mean for telephone surveys. Retrieved from www.pewresearch.org/methods/2017/05/15/what-low-response-rates-mean-for-telephone-surveys/

skilljar, What is customer education? Retrieved from www.skilljar.com/customer-education/

Suh, M., Greene, H., Israilov, B., & Rho, T. (2015). The impact of customer education on customer loyalty through service quality. *Services Marketing Quarterly,* 36(3), 261–280. doi:10.1080/15332969.2015.1046776

Survey Anyplace. (2021). What's the average survey response rate? Benchmark. Retrieved from https://surveyanyplace.com/blog/average-survey-response-rate/

Swinscoe, A. (2010). Are you not getting many customer complaints but are still losing customers? Retrieved from www.adrianswinscoe.com/2010/05/not-many-complaints-but-still-losing-customers/

Section 2

A Roadmap for Proactive Personalized Post-Sales Service

In the first part of the book, we laid out the foundation and the vision for proactive personalized post-sales service (PPPS). We saw how important it is for companies to be next to their customers while they are creating value, and we discussed the three elements a good post-sales program should have: proactive, personalized, and scalable.

In the second part of the book, we will outline how companies can get there. The very short answer to what you need to have in place to do PPPS is the ability to predict customer behavior and the skill to influence it to help customers create more value, and the capacity to do it at scale. I will try to show you that each of these elements is within our reach; if not today, then it will be tomorrow.

I have aimed to summarize the process most businesses follow to design their PPPS programs and the challenges they face along the way in as non-technical language as possible. Yet, I felt that it is better to offer a more in-depth discussion for certain elements, and I have done so.

DOI: 10.4324/9781003309284-6

4 Is Human Behavior Predictable?

Is Human Behavior Predictable?

Hari Seldon was extremely smart, and as chance would have it, also a wise man. He was born and raised in poverty to a father who worked as a tobacco producer and a mother, of whom we know very little. As a young boy, Seldon showed two talents: martial arts and mathematics; the former would come in handy in his life spent in danger; the latter would make him one of the most influential men in history.

In a fictional story born in the mind of Isaac Asimov, Seldon is the protagonist in Asimov's Foundation series, a man with a strong belief in science and rational thinking and their power to help resolve conflicts and build a better world. The Foundation tells the story of a decaying Galactic Empire and the struggle to create a new, better one. In its waning days, the Galactic Empire is home to more than 500 quadrillion citizens, occupying 25 million planets and made possible by hyperspace travel. Existing for over 12,000 years, it is finally coming to an end, losing control over the barbaric kingdoms that thrive in its periphery and civil war tearing its core.

This is when Hari Seldon takes center stage. He develops what is known as psychohistory, or a kind of mathematical sociology, which can predict the behavior of large masses of people. Using it, he foresees the fall of the Empire. He devises a way to lay the foundations of a new empire, preserving the spirit of science and non-violence and shortening the eminent period of chaos between the two. The only caveat is that the people whose behavior psychohistory predicts cannot be aware of the prediction – if they do, their actions become unpredictable.

Science fiction? Yes, most certainly. Right now, we have no way of predicting the actions of so many people so far away in the future – predictions are always probability based. As actions unfold in a sequence, probabilities stack on top of each other, increasing the chance of getting it wrong just two or three steps into the future.

But is psychohistory correct in its basic principles? Is human behavior predictable to a limited extent? Also, most certainly yes.

Perhaps humankind's biggest and most cherished dream is knowing what will happen tomorrow, maybe only challenged by the desire to fly. From

DOI: 10.4324/9781003309284-7

antiquity to the present day, we've always wanted to know what will happen tomorrow, using methods as diverse as "water divining, astrology, numerology, fortune-telling, interpretation of dreams, and many other forms of divination" (Wikipedia.org). With little success, of course.

Then, the scientific method slowly but steadily took hold. With tightly controlled measurements, rigorous analysis, and a community to validate and regulate the process, in the hard sciences domains like biology, chemistry, astronomy, physics, and others, we quickly started to gain reliable, falsifiable, and replicable knowledge about the natural world.

Social sciences quickly followed suit and modeled themselves after the hard sciences. Experimentation and quantitative analysis quickly became the norm in economics, psychology, and sociology. Clearly, the nature of what is being studied is vastly different, which also impacts the scope of research. For example, mixing two chemical compounds and observing the results is very far from observing how a newly married couple raises their kids. Needless to say, you have very limited opportunities to step in the latter to test what impact different interventions might have.

The acceleration of our capabilities to create data and the proliferation of 'breadcrumb' data solve a major challenge for social scientists – getting sufficient and appropriate input in their models. Due to improvements and miniaturization of technology, it is now possible to create data in a much less invasive way than before. However, we don't need to create data in many cases – we can follow people's steps and collect it.

Before we delve into the intricacies of starting and running a successful proactive personalized post-sales service (PPPS) program, I'd like to share some of the most impressive pieces of predictive analytics applied to human behavior. One of the reasons for giving these examples is to showcase how seemingly unpredictable things like selfie popularity or musical preference can be predicted. The second reason to discuss these is to give you a glimpse of the process of doing this. In its very short form, it includes ideation (formulating a hypothesis about the possible relationships between things), getting the data, and running the analysis.

Knowing Where You Are

To an outside observer, our movement patterns can appear random and unpredictable during the data collection. Of course, they are not such to us because we have our motivations to move around the way we do. A group of scientists asked themselves, is our movement truly unpredictable, or is there a pattern to it that can be discerned? To understand this, they obtained three months of location data for 50,000 people from a telco company. The patterns they discovered look quite random, but they are not. In fact, there is a "93% average predictability in user mobility, an exceptionally high value rooted in the inherent regularity of human behavior" (Song et al., 2010, 1018). I think we need to let this sink for a bit. Ninety-three percent of all the places you go are predictable by observing three months of your location data. We are very different from each other; some of us travel far, others do not; some explore new places, and others stick to what they know. However, researchers were able to predict the whereabouts of everyone in the dataset, with at least 80% accuracy. We can predict the trajectory of even the most unpredictable among us with very decent certainty.

Predicting the Next Hit Song

We often think of musical preferences as something deeply personal and contextual. In a lot of ways, they are. At least I am not aware of a model that can say which song I want to listen to right now. Yet, the individuality of our musical taste is also quite a bit of an exaggeration. Many studies in the domain of what is known as Hit Song Science show that song success is very much predictable.

In one of the first attempts at this, Dorien Herremans and her collaborators (Herremans et al., 2014) compiled a database of dance hit songs from 1985 to 2013. For each song, they either extracted or added information classified into three groups:

- Meta-information, like artist location and familiarity
- Basic song features like tempo, mode (major or minor), key, and loudness
- Temporal features: timbre and time between beats

The researchers wanted to know whether these song features could predict song position in music charts, so they also added this information to the database. Once done, they ended up with about 3,500 songs. Next, and we won't go there to save all of us the technical details, they tested various models for predicting song position based on its basic and temporal features. Eventually, they were able to correctly predict the hit status of a song (hit or not a hit) with 64% accuracy, increasing to 83% if one looks within certain subsections of the results alone; for example, the algorithm the researchers developed was able to predict 209 out of a total of 243 hits correctly.

Similarly, to continue with the Hit Song Science example, in early 2021, Adit Kaneria and his collaborators published the results of a project aiming "to predict if a song will be universally recognized using features and attributes of that song which can be quantified using machine learning" (Kaneria et al., 2021). They downloaded features of hit and non-hit songs from Spotify; these include danceability, key, loudness, mode, speechiness, valence (cheerfulness and positivity), and many others. They compared these features against official song charts, and more specifically, whether a song made it to the top 100 or not. Their model was able to achieve an accuracy of 89%. That is, for 9 out of 10 songs, they could tell whether the song would make it to the top 100 list or not.

Predicting Which Images You Would Like

What we said about the individuality of musical preferences perhaps applies even more strongly to images, and we seem to be very confident in the uniqueness of our visual taste. As much as I'd be happy to accept that, a plethora of studies in computer vision seems to defy it. In fact, when we look at images, how memorable they are and how much we like them is quite predictable using artificial intelligence.

In 2014, Aditya Khosla and his collaborators (Khosla et al., 2014) reported the results of a project they conducted to predict how many views a photo would get on social media and photo-sharing websites. First, they collected 2.3 million images from Flickr. Next, they created variables or ways to describe each image. These include "simple human-interpretable features such as color and intensity variance" (Khosla et al., 2014, 870), low-level computer vision features like gradient and texture, and high-level ones like whether various objects were present in the image.[1] The researchers also added social cues, like the number of contacts of the user uploading the photo and membership duration.

With these image and social characteristics, Khosla et al. built a model that gives a high correlation between predicted and actual view count of the photographs (0.81), indicating that it is completely viable to predict people's visual preferences. Similarly, Ke et al. (2006) achieved an accuracy of 72% in distinguishing between high- and low-quality photographs using only image features they extracted automatically from the photos. Lastly, three scientists from the University of Virginia developed an algorithm that can predict with 72% accuracy whether your selfie will become popular.

Predicting Stock Markets Ups and Downs and Whether You'll Default on Your Loan

All investors' dream is to know what will happen on the stock market tomorrow. There are, of course, dozens of models trying to do exactly that. In one of the most creative investigations of stock market up and down movements, three scientists, Bollen, Mao, and Zeng, looked at general mood, as measured by Twitter feeds and analyzed via "the OpinionFinder and GPOMS mood time series" (Bollen et al., 2011, 1). They developed a database of close to 10 million Twitter posts by about 2.7 million users (posted in 2008). They ran the data through text analytics software programs to identify the mood of these feeds. Next to these, they added information about Dow Jones Industrial Average closing-values for the same period. As it turns out, one can, if not fully predict Dow Jones Industrial Average based on the moods of Tweets, then at least improve existing models significantly. In the authors' words, "changes in the public mood state can indeed be tracked from the content of large-scale Twitter feeds using rather simple text processing techniques and that such changes respond to a variety of socio-cultural drivers in a highly differentiated manner" (Bollen et al., 2011, 7).

Staying in the financial domain, in 2019, Netzer, Lemaire, and Herzenstein presented "empirical evidence that borrowers, consciously or not, leave traces of their intentions, circumstances, and personality traits in the text they write when applying for a loan" (Netzer et al., 2019, 960). Adding this information that (potential) customers provide when applying for a loan to models predicting loan default can improve them considerably and yield a 5.75% higher return on investment (compared to models based on financial and demographic information alone). And if you are interested in which words are used by people who default on loans more than those who repay their debt, here they are:

- Words related to financial ('child support,' 'refinance') and general hardships ('stress,' 'divorce')
- "Words that explain their situation (e.g., 'loan explain,' 'explain why') and discuss their work state (e.g., 'hard work')"
- "Appreciative and good-manner words toward lenders (e.g., 'God bless,' 'hello') and pleading lenders for help (e.g., 'need help')"
- Words related to others, like 'son' and 'someone'
- Words related to the short-term, e.g., 'a month'

Getting to Know You by Tracking Your Gaze

As the last example, and one that I particularly enjoy, let's have a brief look at a study Sabrina Hoppe and her collaborators did at Flinders University in South Australia. They had 50 students and staff at the school to "walk around campus for approximately 10 min and to purchase any items of their choice (such as a drink or confectionary) from a campus shop of their choice" (Hoppe et al., 2018), with a "head-mounted video-based eye tracker from SensorMotoric Instruments (SMI)" (Hoppe et al., 2018). After they completed the task, participants were asked to complete a questionnaire which measured the Big Five personality traits, as well as a trait called perceptual curiosity (how interested you are in perceptual stimulation).

Amazingly, using machine-learning methods, the researchers were able to reliably link (with above-chance accuracy) the two pieces of data – you can deduce where a person stands on four of the Big Five traits by looking at where they look during everyday activities. Yes, "an individual's level of neuroticism, extraversion, agreeableness, conscientiousness, and perceptual curiosity can be predicted only from eye movements recorded during an everyday task" (Hoppe et al., 2018). While the accuracy of their model was not huge (at the time of reporting the experiment), it is still remarkable how creative thinking to formulate an interesting hypothesis, efforts to collect the right data, and knowledge of the state-of-the-art data analytics methods can do combined.

A Process of Delivering PPPS

What we saw so far are truly remarkable pieces of analytics expanding the universe of our knowledge for ourselves, and we focused a bit more on the process, and the types of data researchers used to develop them. I believe it is a very similar process that can help your company design and implement a successful PPPS program.

I'm not going to try to sugarcoat it for you. Getting from the existing modes of delivering post-sales service to a proactive and personalized one, and doing it at scale, could be a challenge. Like anything that hasn't become mainstream yet, companies will be figuring it out on the go. Still, it is also not an insurmountable challenge, as the success story of Liberty Global and the plethora of other examples we saw earlier show. All you need to get there is the right data, the cutting-edge analytics to predict customer behavior, and the willingness and capabilities to act.

I believe that every company can start doing PPPS by following a process similar to the one below and described in Figure 4.1.

1   Kick-off. Set goals, get buy-in, and plan
2   Input: collect customer feedback. This is part 1 of the data you'll use to create the predictive algorithms later
3   Input: collect customer data and fuse it all. Customer data is the second element of the data you'll use to create the predictive algorithms later on. And if you can't link it all together, you have no way of understanding the relationship between customer feedback and customer data, rendering predictive analytics impossible
4   Understanding: run analytics to recognize the pattern of behavior that indicates dissatisfaction or suboptimal value-creation
5   Action: learn how to intervene in the process and embed it in the company's day-to-day operations, monitor the results, and adjust as needed
6   Scale-up: predict what you don't know and expand the service to your full customer base

Figure 4.1 The process of designing and implementing a proactive personalized post-sales service program.

As you can see, this is a fairly standard process going from planning, through getting the right input in, through analyzing what you have gathered, to taking action and monitoring the results. Indeed, there is nothing overly complex in the process itself. Without knowing your organization, I will still make the reasonable prediction that you are doing most if not all of these things already. You could be doing it in a suboptimal way, or you could be covering only part of your customers, or you could be lacking the data analytics capabilities to create the algorithms. That is not an uncommon place to be in – in reality, very few companies have all the elements in place. What is important is that you've already made inroads into each of these areas, so there will be nothing new for you.

What is different in this process is what you are aiming for, and that is supporting your customers in a proactive and personalized way while they are creating value with your product or service, and all of that, in a scalable fashion. In the following subchapters, we will look at each of these in turn, discuss the purpose at each step, what I believe you should be aiming for as an outcome, and how to do it, including best practices and real-life examples.

Note

1 As an aside, the objects with the highest positive impact on image views are "miniskirt, maillot, bikini, cup, brassiere, perfume, revolver", while those with the lowest – "spatula, plunger, laptop, golfcart, space heater". Why would someone photograph a spatula is beyond me but hey, I don't judge!

References

Bollen, J., Mao, H., & Zeng, X.-J. (2011). Twitter mood predicts the stock market. *Journal of Computational Science*, 2(1), 1–8. doi:10.1016/j.jocs.2010.12.007

Herremans, D., Martens, D., & Sörensen, K. (2014). Dance hit song prediction. *Journal of New Music Research*, 43(3), 291–302. doi:10.1080/09298215.2014.881888

Hoppe, S., Loetscher, T., Morey, S. A., & Bulling, A. (2018). Eye movements during everyday behavior predict personality traits. *Frontiers in Human Neuroscience*, 12, 105. doi:10.3389/fnhum.2018.00105. Retrieved from www.frontiersin.org/artic les/10.3389/fnhum.2018.00105/full

Kaneria, A.V., Rao, A. B., Aithal, S. G., & Pai, S. N. (2021). Prediction of song popularity using machine learning concepts. In K.V. S. Rao (Ed.) K. (eds), *Smart sensors measurements and instrumentation*, Lecture notes in electrical engineering, 750. Singapore: Springer. doi:10.1007/978-981-16-0336-5_4

Ke, Y., Tang, X., & Jing, F. (2006). The design of high-level features for photo quality assessment. IEEE Computer Society Conference on Computer Vision and Pattern Recognition (CVPR2006) (pp. 419–426). doi:10.1109/CVPR.2006.303

Khosla, A., Das Sarma, A., & Hamid, R. (2014). What makes an image popular? In Proceedings of the 23rd International Conference on World Wide Web (WWW 2014) (pp. 867–876). New York, NY: Association for Computing Machinery. doi:10.1145/2566486.2567996

Netzer, O., Lemaire, A., & Herzenstein, M. (2019). When words sweat: Identifying signals for loan default in the text of loan applications. *Journal of Marketing Research*, 56(6), 960–980. doi:10.1177/0022243719852959

Song, C., Qu, Z., Blumm, N., & Barabási, A. L. (2010 February 19). Limits of predictability in human mobility. *Science*, 327(5968), 1018–1021. doi:10.1126/science.1177170, PMID: 20167789

Wikipedia.org. Prediction. Retrieved from https://en.wikipedia.org/wiki/Prediction

5   Roadmap Step 1 – Kick-Off

Set Goals, Plan, and Get Buy-In

What Is the Purpose of This Stage?

Proactive personalized post-sales service (PPPS) is, to a large extent, a vision for how the company does business and interacts with its customers. Like any vision, achieving it is not a trivial matter – it is going to be a process. On the positive side, it is a process just like any other you have in your company, and it is something that you can prepare for.

In a nutshell, the purpose of this very first stage of doing PPPS is to set yourself up for success. What I've seen in practice is that this includes three crucial steps: setting clear goals, making a plan for achieving these, and getting buy-in from the stakeholders the execution depends on.

Ideally, at the end of this stage, I believe you would have clear answers to questions such as these:

- Do I know what I want the company to achieve in the domain of PPPS? If I show this vision to someone who hadn't been involved in this, would they understand it? Would they be inspired?
- Can you clearly see the relationships between specific actions or initiatives and the goal of becoming an organization that proactively addresses customer needs?
- Do I know what we need to do tomorrow, in a week, or three months? Are there clear milestones in place? Do I have an idea of the kind of resources I would need?
- Do the people this execution depends on support this vision? Would they invest in it? If there is a clash between PPPS and other priorities, would they support PPPS?

Goal Setting and Planning

In my practice and the writings of others, I've found that a critical first step in the process is defining what you are aiming for. The goal-setting literature itself is vast, and we can't cover all the elements of what a good goal-setting process looks like, but we can touch on a few important ones.

DOI: 10.4324/9781003309284-8

First things first, what are goals? Psychologically speaking, a goal is "… a mental representation of a desired end state that a person is committed to approaching or avoiding" (Höchli et al., 2018). It is the vision in our minds of what we want to do (or avoid). In fact, many renowned psychologists would go as far as to claim that all human behavior is goal-driven. This is not to say that we always have conscious awareness of our goals, but it points out that everything we do has a purpose.

Goals serve a very important function in our mental lives: they channel our energy and behavior in the desired direction. It is difficult to imagine a life without goals, even the simplest ones like getting to work or buying yogurt, but if we try, we'll only see chaos and randomness or complete and utter apathy. Without something to direct our actions, we will be at the mercy of all the forces surrounding us, physical or social. It is only through goals that we can organize our behavior in at least a relatively consistent and coherent manner.

In organizations, goals serve the very same purpose, for they are, like human beings, akin to what is known in cybernetics as negative-feedback loops. The latter is a simple concept really: a negative-feedback loop monitors the environment for a specific parameter, compares it with a reference value, and if the input deviates from the latter, initiates an action to close this gap. This dance between goals, actual values, and actions never stops in neither human nor organizations – otherwise, no activity will ever occur. Crucially though, this process presupposes the existence of a goal, or input, and of the ability to take action. If one of these elements were removed, nothing would ever happen.

There are several ways in which we can describe goals. They could be long-term or short-term, positive (I want to achieve) or negative (I want to avoid), driven by intrinsic or extrinsic motivations, mastery (improve competence) or achievement (gain the respect or approval of others), challenging or not, and of course, goals could be more or less specific. The latter is a crucial distinction, and it has become customary in business contexts to state that goals should be specific and measurable. I agree with this, but I also find it limiting, as these goals can easily lead to shortsightedness and "compensatory effects that undermine goal pursuit in the long run" (Höchli et al., 2018).

The best way I know of taking the best of both worlds, having specific and more abstract goals, is the goal hierarchy approach, brilliantly described by Bettina Höchli and her collaborators (2018). It states that goals exist on a tree-like continuum from the simplest and very specific ones at the bottom (subordinate goals) to the broadest, abstract ones at the top (super-ordinate goals), and laying out the full picture can give the best of both worlds and help mitigate the downsides of having only very specific or only very abstract goals.

At the top are identity-based goals. These define who we want to be, hence why they are sometimes called be-goals. At this level, we describe what is important for us in life. "I want to be healthy", "I want to be rich", or "I want to be a winner" are all good examples of these. Be-goals are long-term and are very often abstract (i.e., less specific). They could also be quite difficult to measure; for example, being healthy is a difficult thing to define – is there an end state of health, or is there always something more you can do?

These superordinate, or be-goals, give rise to more specific, more measurable intermediate goals, which we can call do-goals. They "provide a general course of action that is bound to a certain behavioral context" (Höchli et al., 2018), i.e., what are the things that I want to do to achieve my be-goals? What does a person who is healthy do? What does a person who is rich do? In a nutshell, these are more concrete but still programmatic actions one can take to achieve their superordinate goals. These are not yet single action things but instead consist of multiple acts one should take to achieve them.

Finally, at the bottom, you have the subordinate goals which

> define precisely what to do and how to do it. By taking into account environmental affordances and constraints, they specify concretely how goals one step up in the hierarchy—that is, intermediate goals—can be achieved (Boekaerts et al., 2006)
>
> (Höchli et al., 2018)

For the purpose of PPPS, we will refer to this lowest level of goals as plans – the specific things you are planning to do to achieve the intermediate goals and thus the superordinate or be-goals.

Laying out the full structure of goals gives you some very important benefits. On the one hand, it increases the meaningfulness of what one does. If you focus on the lowest level or the subordinate goals, it is very easy to forget why you are doing what you are doing. In fact, several studies show that the question Why moves people up in the hierarchy, while the question How moves them down. Both are beneficial, yet given that our daily lives mostly happen via mundane activities specified at the lowest level, it is worth enhancing the meaning of these banal actions by remembering what they lead to.

A second benefit of having this whole tree-like structure in front of you is that it guides you and helps you prioritize. If your be-goal is to become an organization that proactively addresses customer needs, then all the goals below should stem from this purpose. And the logical question to ask every time a new initiative comes up is, is this helping me achieve this? How would this initiative move my organization closer to proactively addressing customer needs?

Superordinate goals, or be-goals, also help you be more focused and resilient. Studies show that when people think of their goals in higher-level terms, they are more likely to sustain effort and have a healthy disregard for what's easy in favor of what's right.

Finally, and somewhat unexpectedly, remembering superordinate goals also makes us more flexible and enhances creativity. What we typically refer to as out-of-the-box thinking is often better described as moving up and then down again in the hierarchy of goals. A British expression sums it up well – there are many ways to skin a cat. This way of thinking is unlocked by moving slightly up the hierarchy to remind oneself of the goal; from this vantage point, more solutions might become visible, enhancing flexibility.

The best advice I can give you when setting up a PPPS program is to create exactly this kind of goal hierarchy. Again, it will help you stay focused, guide your efforts, and make you more flexible in your approach.

As an example, a good be-goal for PPPS could be something similar to "We want to be an organization that proactively addresses customer needs in a personalized fashion". At the second level, the intermediate goals could very well be the process we described at the beginning of this section. You will need good measurement, analytics, and actions to make it happen. Finally, at the bottom layer, you would lay out the specific steps you will take. We will look at these in the chapters that follow, but as an example, the goal of measuring current customer experience (CX) could be achieved by setting up a CX survey, for which you need (a) a platform, (b) a questionnaire, (c) analytical plan, (d) a dashboard to disseminate the results, etc. When you add dates and responsible parties to it, this layer will also constitute your plan for becoming an organization that proactively addresses customer needs.

We need to make one final point here: this goal map is a living document. For example, you can lay out a fairly complete plan for getting input and analyzing the results. However, the action stages will depend on the execution of these, and you can't plan for them in advance. What you can do is to have placeholders, such as running an action-discovery session; after you hold this session, you can move on to specifying the rest of the actions.

Getting Buy-In

Whatever position you hold in a business, you will always need to get people's buy-in for action; even the most autocratic regimes do that – coercion and violence are ways to get buy-in, albeit not ones that we appreciate. Even if you are the CEO, you would need motivated and willing people to act on the vision you've come up with. And things become even more difficult in the middle of organizations, where you would have to work with people higher, lower, and at the same level in the hierarchy as you. What can you do to move people in your direction? How to do change management at scale – upwards, downwards, and across?

It is beyond the scope of this book to offer an extensive discussion on the topic, but I'd still like to propose two things that help tremendously in the process. I adapt from the leadership guru John Kotter to create a sense of urgency and build and maintain a guiding coalition (Kotter Inc. and Kotter, 2012). Getting buy-in to a very large extent is about having the right content and a good network to support you in the execution. Creating a sense of urgency is vital as it leads to very different actions than ones driven by complacency or disengagement. In the words of Kotter,

When people have a true sense of urgency, they think that action on critical issues is needed now, not eventually, not when it fits easily into a schedule.... A sense of urgency is not an attitude that I must have the project team meeting today, but that the meeting must accomplish something important today.

Kotter offers four tactics for generating this impetus for action:

Bring the Outside In. The goal of bringing the outside in is to fight companies' tendency to focus on how they work internally rather than on what's happening in the broader ecosystem. In my view, a crucial part of the outside-in perspective is the customers' (incl. prospects) view of the company. CX studies help tremendously in this task, be they in focus groups, large-scale studies, or user-generated content analysis. And don't forget that you have a major, often untapped, source of information for customers – your customer-interfacing employees. While not always objective, they will still provide a plethora of insights you can complement with more impartial views from surveys or other analyses. An important point Kotter makes, and one to which I fully subscribe, is not to shield people from troubling data, or at least not always. This is in line with Ray Dalio's advice to practice radical transparency. I'm a firm believer in this for one simple reason: if we don't provide people with enough information, how do we expect them to make the right decisions? No one stands to benefit from us not sharing the results from customer satisfaction studies with a wide audience within the company. I recommend companies to spread the word, no matter if it's positive or negative. Other tactics that help bring the outside in include the power of video, bringing people in, and sending people out. The last two, I find to be underutilized by companies: rarely do I hear my clients saying that they visited competitors' stores just to check what they are offering; and rarely do I see real customers in meeting rooms with customer experience teams, for example. Both are very effective techniques because they are really simple to implement and can move the proverbial needle significantly.

Behave with Urgency Every Day. The name of this tactic says much about what it is. It is unreasonable to expect that if we don't behave with a sense of urgency, we can inspire others to do so. Every individual can incite and lead a change management effort, and this is the crux of the matter – show others how you think the company should act.

There are several things you can do to lead by example. For one thing, Kotter says, "purge and delegate". Get rid of unproductive activities and focus on what makes an impact. Set your agenda as much as you can. Clear your schedule, so you have the time to jump in when needed. Oh, and manage the meetings so they end up with clear action plans – who will do what when; unless you have that, you don't have an action plan. Easier said than done, I know; nevertheless, a reminder for all of us to focus on what works instead of what's habitual.

You can put this time you just freed up in your calendar to talk to people, call customers, gather outside information, and do other activities that promote your cause. Perhaps most importantly, make all of this visible, Kotter says. The goal isn't to create buzz for the sake of it – no one likes that. Rather, the goal is to draw your colleagues' attention to the matter and spark their interest. Success breeds success – the more successful you are, the more people will want to join your cause.

Find Opportunities in Crisis. Disruptions to our daily lives are painful, especially when they come with an enormous loss of human lives. Nevertheless, crisis times also open opportunities to become better at what we do, or simply put – to become better people. Why so? Because they rupture the tissue of everyday life and expose what's beneath. They draw our attention and make us look at things like we never did before. They make us ask questions on why and how things like that are. They make us explore what's out there instead of exploiting what we have. In the memorable words of Rahm Emanuel, "You never want a serious crisis to go to waste".

This is exactly the point of view John Kotter is advocating. To instill a sense of urgency in our companies, we need to use what crises give us – a window of opportunity to change the typical way we do things. There are two recommendations Kotter gives for using a crisis to create a sense of urgency that I particularly appreciate:

- "To use a crisis to reduce complacency, make sure it is visible, unambiguous, related to real business problems, and significant enough that it cannot be solved with small, simple actions. Fight the impulse to minimize or hide bad news" (Kotter, 2008, 142).
- "To use a crisis to reduce complacency, be exceptionally proactive in assessing how people will react, in developing specific plans for action, and in implementing the plans swiftly" (Kotter, 2008, 142).

And then, you also have the option to create a crisis instead of waiting for one to happen. Of course, this is risky and should be used sparingly, but it's worth mentioning here as it's still a viable option. Either way, a customer experience crisis represents a major opportunity to draw the attention of coworkers to this vital element of a company's offering. We will do well to see it and use it as such.

Deal with the NoNos. And finally, there are always people who will fight on the side of the status quo. No matter how much you try to convince them and how many data points you share, these people consistently refuse to accept the facts, for example, that customer experience is vital for building a viable business.

Jonah Berger offers some great advice for changing anyone's mind in his book, The Catalyst (Berger, 2020); in short, Berger urges us to work to remove the five obstacles that stop people from changing:

- Reactance: an action has an equal and opposite reaction. You push people, and people push back. To tackle this challenge, "allow for agency". The goal here is to give people a choice; Jonah Berger puts it well, "...let people pick the path. Let them choose how they get where you are hoping they'll go" (Berger, 2020, 30). Also, whenever possible, opt for questions instead of answers. The answers are almost always obvious if you pose the right question. And questions have an added benefit – they expand people's perspectives, and you may end up having more ideas than in the beginning. Another good advice for tackling Reactance is to highlight the gap, but I'd add an important caveat – show, don't tell. For example, can you have a customer talk about his experience while pitching your idea? Can you send your colleagues a single review a customer has given you every day? Bring the real-life into the board room, and real-life will serve you well.

- Endowment: we like it easy, so we stick with what we are doing. Unless there is a good reason for it, we tend to do what we've always done. One powerful action you can take is to clarify the cost of inaction. Framing things in terms of losses is very powerful. What will happen if you don't act on improving CX? Will you lose this customer in 6 months? Will the customer lifetime value (CLTV) decrease by 20%? You can figure this out; once you do, use it to create a sense of urgency.

- Distance: we like to work within our zones of acceptance. New information that is within it can land well but push too far; it has no chance of success. Berger's advice is to go small and 'ask for less.' Remember that the distance roadblock exists because there is a large gap between your point of view and how the person you are convincing to do something sees the world. Also, remember that there is always an overlap between you two, no matter how far you are. Use this 'movable middle' to find common ground. And don't ask for much – ask for a pilot, a start, a small change today, and then in one week, ask for another. Small is beautiful.

- Uncertainty: if we are unsure of the outcome, we are unlikely to act. One thing we can do to navigate this roadblock is to give a trial option. By now, this is a very popular way of managing uncertainty, given that you can get a demo or a short-term subscription to any piece of software. In essence, anything that helps people try something without committing to it helps.

- Corroborating Evidence: we need more than anecdotal evidence; we need many people to show us or tell us something to start believing it. If you can show that a similar company has done something similar in a similar situation, that will be golden. Or look for examples internally – has a colleague of yours done something that improved CX significantly? How can you celebrate this success? How can you tie success within the company with customer success?

Maybe none of the tactics described here won't be enough to get buy-in for your initiatives, or maybe they will. Either way, it is worth giving it a go if you care about the sustainable growth of your company. Try to show your people where the world is headed; try to show them how they are currently doing some of these things – it's not entirely new. Celebrate success together with them, and of course, whatever you do, keep in mind that showing the financial impact of these initiatives is very often the key ingredient for success. Start now, act with urgency, form a coalition, and success is very likely to come your way. Others are already doing it.

References

Berger, J. (2020). *The catalyst: How to change anyone's mind.* Kindle Edition. Simon and Schuster.

Höchli, B., Brügger, A., & Messner, C. (2018). How focusing on superordinate goals motivates broad, long-term goal pursuit: A theoretical perspective. *Frontiers in Psychology*, 9, 1879. doi:10.3389/fpsyg.2018.01879. Retrieved from www.frontier sin.org/articles/10.3389/fpsyg.2018.01879/full

Kotter, Inc. The 8-step process for leading change. Retrieved from www.kotterinc. com/8-step-process-for-leading-change/

Kotter, J. (2008). *A sense of urgency.* Kindle Edition. Harvard Business Review Press. Boston, Massachusetts.

Kotter, J. P. (2012). Accelerate! *Harvard Business Review*, 90(11), 44–52, 54. Retrieved from https://hbr.org/2012/11/accelerate

6 Roadmap Step 2 – Input
Collect Customer Feedback

Now that you are on the road toward doing proactive personalized post-sales service (PPPS), it is time to get things rolling. Talking about data collection could be seen as boring for some, and I'd gladly skip this part if it hadn't been the foundation for everything that you'll be doing later. I don't believe anyone wants to put something as important as the support you'll provide your customers in their quest to create value on shaky grounds.

With this in mind, the first thing to do if you are starting from scratch is to ensure that you have the right data. This is the topic of this and the next two chapters – why and how to collect customer feedback, customer behavioral and transactional data, and why and how to fuse them.

What Is the Purpose of This Stage?

There are many benefits of collecting customer feedback data. It can be used to improve products or services at large, input for 360-degree employee evaluation, or run close-the-loop programs. In the context of PPPS, customer feedback is one of the sides of the equation you are looking to solve, so it's vital to get it right.

What does 'getting customer feedback collection right' mean in our context? Here are four suggestions for must-haves: good customer feedback collection is as valid as possible, reliable, covers customers' evaluation of the company or a specific product or service on overall key performance indicator (KPI) and customers' reasons for evaluating the company the way they did. Additionally, the feedback from specific customers can be linked to their behavioral and transactional data.

Must-Haves

Validity and reliability are both common prerequisites for almost everything data-related that you will ever do, and it's never too much to say a couple of words about them. In a nutshell, both of these items concern the level of trust you can have in the results; how certain are you that what you have collected as customer feedback is the actual customer feedback.

DOI: 10.4324/9781003309284-9

Data validity is about the accuracy of measurement. For example, a weighting scale that says something weighs 1 km while in reality, it weighs 0.5 kg is not delivering valid measurement. Now, the question is, how do you know that it weighs 1.0 kg in the first place? And this is an especially troubling question in sampling research. If you have done studies on your entire customer base, you would already have a benchmark to compare to, but this defies the purpose of doing sampling research and is, in most cases, practically impossible. This latter consideration is an important aspect of data validity known as generalizability. These are the results you obtain from the part of the customer base you are surveying representative of the whole customer base.

Two ways help estimate the validity of data for our purposes, and unfortunately, none of them can give you an ultimate answer. You can compare how your results stack up against "existing theory and knowledge of the concept being measured" (Middleton, 2019). For example, if you measure overall customer satisfaction and customer satisfaction on certain aspects, say, price, quality, and durability, you expect that at least some of the latter correlate strongly with the former. If this is not the case, you could start raising questions about the validity of the results.

A second way to estimate data validity is to compare to other known measurements of the same thing. For example, if you know that customer satisfaction leads to loyalty, then a good measurement of the former would correlate with the latter. It is exactly this relationship that we are often not certain of, so it is difficult to use it as a criterion for validity. These difficulties aside, there are ways in which you can increase the probability that you are collecting valid results, and we'll talk about them in the second section of this chapter.

The second consideration to have in mind when collecting customer feedback is data reliability. It is related to validity, but while the latter is about accuracy, reliability is about consistency. The key question here is, if you do a second measurement at exactly the same time with the same group of people and in the same context, will you get the same results? The major challenge with estimating reliability is that you cannot, with some exceptions, do this in the social world. Even if you survey the same people one hour apart, you might already be studying them under different conditions – they moved around, got angry or happy, etc. Furthermore, many people would get irritated by being asked the same things so close in time.

Having ensured that your customer feedback collection meets the formal data validity and reliability criteria, what exactly do you measure? In other words, assuming that you are doing this via a customer survey, what do you include in the questionnaire?

My advice is to go as simple as possible and, if needed, expand later by doing deep-dive measurements or adding further questions. The rationale behind this recommendation stems from the minimum requirements for running the analytics that will unlock a successful PPPS program. You need two things – an overall evaluation of your company, product, or service by customers and their reasons for giving this evaluation.

The overall evaluation will later become the thing you are going to predict. At this point, except in some special cases, because of practical considerations and the survey response iceberg, you are collecting the feedback of only some customers. To truly do PPPS, you need feedback from all customers, which means that you have to predict the feedback of the remainder of your customers. This is the reason for including the overall measurement here – it will serve as the thing to be predicted at later stages.

In practice, it might even be enough only to have this overall evaluation. Yet, my advice is also to ask customers about the reasons for their evaluation. Without elaborating further on what is likely an obvious observation, knowing that your customers think highly or not of you is excellent, but what is better is knowing why they think it. Otherwise, when you start trying to intervene and propose improvements, you wouldn't be basing them on solid ground and risk scattering them. We'll talk more about how to achieve this in the second part of this chapter, and we'll touch upon how you can analyze the drivers of the evaluation later on.

The fourth element I suggest that you consider when designing your customer feedback collection is whether you can link it with the behavioral and transactional data you have for customers. This is also a vital part of the prediction process. In earlier chapters, we spoke about customer complaints and survey response icebergs. Both of these are metaphors for the fact that you will be unable to get the opinion of all of your customers – neither by letting them, nor encouraging them to contact you if they encounter issues nor by you reaching out to them. To solve this, you would be using the feedback you've managed to collect from customers to predict what those who hadn't been in touch with you think. This is only possible if you manage to link survey responses with the data you already have for your customers' behavior and interactions with you. That is why choosing a customer feedback collection method that will allow for this linkage is a must-have if you want to do PPPS; otherwise, you have no way of predicting what all of your customers think and feel.

Advisable-To-Have

Initially, I had added a fourth point to the list of requirements, yet after some deliberation, I decided to remove it. This third criterion concerns monitoring the development of customer feedback in time. Although it's not a hard requirement, I cannot recommend strongly enough to design your customer feedback collection in a manner that allows for it. Collecting customer feedback at multiple points in time unlocks later on the opportunity to monitor the impact of your actions, i.e., linking PPPS initiatives to return on investment (ROI). Without it, there is just no way for you to know whether you moved the proverbial needle or not.

In its hard version, monitoring customer feedback in time is done via 'longitudinal data,' or surveying the same customer several times (with sufficient time between the surveys). The softer and more often practiced version is to collect tracking data – you still collect feedback repeatedly, but not necessarily with the same customers. In reality, your data would very rarely be exclusively longitudinal, as no matter what you do, some customers will stop replying to your survey. Of course, you can replace them, but then you no longer have a full data set. That is why in practice, almost all of the data that you'll work with is tracking data.

Preferably, you would be able to generate enough scale to allow for more accurate algorithms to be developed at a later stage. A good rule of thumb is to look for numbers in the range of 1,000 observations or more, but do not take this as a strict rule, as there are ways to circumnavigate the issue.

I'd advise you not to obsess about having an excellent representation of all of your customers in your feedback collection. That means you don't limit yourself to customers for which you have an email in your Customer Relationship Management (CRM) platform, for example, or to big customers only. In a perfect world, I'd strongly recommend you to do so to make sure that what you are doing is truly applicable to your whole customer base. I suggest that if you can do a little, you'd better do it instead of waiting for the perfect conditions. Just have the caveat that you might be missing the feedback of a substantial (or not) group of your customers.

As a recap, to unlock PPPS, your customer feedback data would be valid, reliable and would cover the KPI you have chosen and the reasons why customers evaluate you in this way. Preferably, you would also have a way to monitor the development of customer feedback in time, and you would have a good enough scale of it (number of observations). Also, preferable, but don't overthink it, is to collect feedback from all types of customers. With this, we turn to a discussion on how to achieve these things.

Practical Advice on Collecting Customer Feedback

The remainder of this chapter is, by necessity, quite technical, as it delves into the intricacies of collecting customer feedback. I felt that it is necessary to include it in this book in the spirit of laying out the full PPPS design and implementation process.

There are many ways to get customer feedback, of which one is best suited to achieve the outcomes we just discussed – running a quantitative survey with your customers. All the other options are extremely valuable, and we'll use them later, but they have certain disadvantages from the perspective of enabling customer prediction. For example, you can analyze what your customers say when they leave a complaint, which will be very insightful. Yet, it violates the principle of validity of data – relying only on the people who leave a complaint will result in a non-representative sample. Another option is to mine customer reviews online. Again, it is an extremely insightful exercise, yet, to the best of my knowledge, there is no way of linking this feedback to your customers' behavioral and transactional data. Another option still is to do qualitative research with your customers. I love qualitative research, and I think it's one of the most helpful things you can do. But in this case, it doesn't allow for the scale you need. And finally, you can do quantitative research in a competitive context, i.e., including your competitors' customers in the study. While also very helpful for certain cases, you can't connect this feedback with your internal data.

This leaves the option of collecting customer feedback via a quantitative study with your customers. The process is straightforward and tried and tested in practice for decades now. Its basic form is the one outlined below. I have offered some basic advice on each stage, and we'll spend more time on a couple of important points in the remainder of this chapter.

- Define the goals of the study: We did this in previous chapters
- Design the study, i.e., develop the methodology you'll be using. There are a couple of important considerations to take into account here:
- Is it going to be an online or telephone survey (or maybe face to face in some markets)? Are you going to reach out to customers via email, phone, or in-person? Typically, in B2C businesses in most markets, you'd do an online study, and B2B businesses would mostly rely on telephone interviews. There are exceptions, of course, and in some industries, we see increasing use of online surveys for B2B audiences as well – healthcare is a good example here.
- What will your sample composition be? The invites sent to customers should share the same structure as your full customer base to ensure representativeness. If you have a 50/50 gender split, make sure that out of the total number of invites you send, 50% go to women and 50% to men. Same with age, region, and all other variables that might be important in your line of business.
- Develop the questionnaire. We will discuss this in more detail below as it's one of the vital steps in this process.
- Prepare the survey for sending to customers, or in technical lingo – script the survey.
- One thing you'd have to decide here is whether to use one of the specialized customer experience measurement and management platforms or not. My advice is to use one if you can, as it will also give you excellent reporting capabilities and the technological foundation to implement a close-the-loop program.
- Often, you'd have to run the survey in one (Switzerland, India) or many markets speaking different languages. Pay special attention to translations, as a poor translation can alter the meaning of your original question and disrupt the validity of your results.
- Prepare the sample, i.e., the list of customers to whom you'd be sending the survey. A critical point here is to make sure that you don't bias the list in any way, for example, by selecting customers that you know are happy.

The goal is not to engage in self-glorification but to practice radical honesty.

- Send the survey or conduct the survey over the phone.
- Run a pilot. I cannot stress how important this is and how often companies overlook it, mostly because of timing considerations. The goal of the pilot is to ensure that you have gotten everything right, and if not, to allow you to improve before you go live with thousands of customers. If you do a bigger pilot, that's even better, as it will allow you to run a pre-analysis of the results and see if you need to make adjustments to the questionnaire. It doesn't take much – neither in terms of time nor investment – so I recommend definitely making an effort.
- Analyze the results. This will be the subject of a whole chapter later on.

The space and purpose of this book don't allow us to go into many more details on collecting customer feedback. Yet, before we close this chapter, I think it's worth spending some time talking about two points in particular: selecting the right KPI, and how to measure the 'Why?' behind customers' evaluation on the KPI.

Choosing the Right KPI

One question I often hear from clients, and I see repeatedly brought up in professional discussions, is what KPI to use as customers' overall evaluation of the company, product, or service. These debates often revolve around two major candidates for the role of customer experience KPIs – Net Promoter Score (NPS) and Overall satisfaction (Rise of the customer experience leader: 2020 research report). In my view, the main reason for the reoccurrence of these discussions is that there is no perfect metric, and in a lot of ways, it doesn't matter too much which one you will use. This might sound odd, or even maybe preposterous, but I'm surely not aiming for either of those. I'm merely pointing out that whether you measure the temperature in degrees Celsius, or Kelvin, or Fahrenheit, you would still only have a hint as to how cold or warm you would feel when you go out. It might take you some time to adjust to the fact that 30 degrees Celsius is warm, but 30 degrees Fahrenheit is cold, yet eventually, you will start dressing appropriately.

The one thing I find important when deciding which KPI to use is that it gives enough space for customers to express their opinion adequately. In a simpler sentence, I'd advise using a wider scale, such as a 7-pt, a 10-pt, or an 11-pt one (like the one used to calculate NPS). Examples would be the scale used to measure NPS (How likely are you to recommend brand X? with answers ranging from 0 – Not at all likely, to 10 – Extremely likely), or an overall customer satisfaction scale with seven possible answers (Overall, how satisfied are you with the products and services provided by company X? with answers ranging from 1 – Extremely dissatisfied to 7 – Extremely satisfied). Such an approach allows for an expression of nuanced feedback without being overwhelming (like using a 100-pt scale, for example).

Beyond that, I find the discussion around whether NPS or Customer Satisfaction (CSAT) works better to be futile. I have seen academic articles showing the former's supremacy and others claiming the opposite. And in my practice, I have seen companies do miracles with CX using NPS, and I've seen others using CSAT and transforming the way they do business. Still, others have used product quality as a KPI, and it has helped them instill a customer-centric culture and make important changes to the customer experience they deliver.

The real difference is how the company works with NPS or CSAT, not whether NPS or CSAT work. Metrics simply guide. Companies and people do the work.

Measuring the 'Why' Behind Customers' Attitude

Now that you have the KPI in place, it's time to allow customers to also share the reasons they evaluate the company the way they do. This is important as it guides company's improvement efforts in the right direction. If I can offer some advice here, it would be to get the best of two worlds – on what you would like customers to evaluate you and what customers want to share with you. To do this, you would need to add two questions.

An Open-Ended Question

The first one would be an open-ended question immediately after the KPI question. Ask customers something like "What are the reasons behind giving this score?" and just give them the space to write down or share their unbiased, spontaneous response. There are many advantages to using this type of question here, the most important being that you can hear/read what customers have to say. The variety of responses will also be greater, and if the customer is sufficiently motivated, you can get much more details and variety in their answer. In many ways, these are akin to the customer reviews on websites we grew used to in recent years. Amazon, for example, allows you to do two things. First, give a rating on a 5-pt scale (or 5 stars); second, write what you think about the product in more detail.

Here's an example of the depth (some) people would go to when leaving a review; I randomly selected one to showcase the richness of detail you can get from an open-ended response and a motivated customer. It is for a Nikon D750 camera:

> The reason I decided to go with a D750 when I already owned the D610 was its superior tracking ability of moving subjects in well-lit and low light conditions. I shoot a lot of wildlife, especially birds in flight, and they are not easy subjects to capture. I also enjoy shooting local live bands in very challenging lighting situations, and while my D610 was handling these conditions pretty well, it did miss a few shots every now and then that I wish I had gotten. Especially when it comes to birds

flying toward me at fast speeds, the D610 could not always keep up with them. The keeper rate was acceptable, but the D750 simply performs better in these situations. I get more keepers, plus I get slightly faster FPS, which means I get slightly more frames to choose from.

In low light, where even my eyes struggle to see any contrast, there is no contest between the two cameras. The D750 locks on in near darkness, whereas the D600/D610 would hunt under the same conditions. As long as there is contrast visible, the D610 will do just fine. I've put it through some difficult circumstances, and it handled them better than I expected. The D750, however, is just more sure of itself. It hunts less, it will lock quickly, and your results will be impressive.

The image quality of the D750 is great of course, just as it is when using the D610. Auto white balance works surprisingly well. Skin tones look nice, and so does everything else. Highlight-weighed metering is an interesting option and helps to preserve whites that might otherwise be blown out.

At first, I felt the flip screen wouldn't do me much good as a still photography shooter, but now that I have it, I do use it to get some odd angles which I wouldn't have gotten otherwise. I'm not always willing to lay on the ground or stand on my tiptoes to get a shot, and now I don't have to. The screen is sturdy and hasn't gotten in the way, so it seems like a pretty useful feature. Fold it in when not in use, bring it out when you need it.

Not only does it perform as promised, but I have also not experienced any negative issues that may have plagued some past Nikon models. I've shot around 5,000 frames with it so far and there are no signs of anything going awry. It focuses fast regardless of light availability, and high ISO photos look great, especially when processed through Lightroom. Basically, if you're looking for an action DSLR with lots of great features for a reasonable price, the D750 will fit you well.

UPDATE: (Some people have reported seeing a shadow band at the top of the frame when shooting flares at specific angles. I have not seen this problem with my D750, but Nikon issued an advisory to repair it for free if you happen to see it. Most have not encountered this problem during normal shooting, only when they intentionally tried to induce this shadow band. If you like to shoot flares or if you shoot a lot of videos, you may want to check your body for the problem when you buy it. Personally, I don't think this is as big of a problem as oil spots on sensor or left focusing issue, but there are a few buyers out there who might be affected by it. Personally, I have not seen this problem with three different D750 bodies I used, but some others might.)

This is not the end of the review – the customer continues by giving you suggestions on what to do if you are a beginner, if you already own a previous model, and so on. To continue this example, the level of detail is comparable to an image taken with a super high-resolution camera – you can zoom in and zoom in almost endlessly and you don't lose any of the picture quality.

There are certain downsides to this open-ended type of asking customers about why they evaluate your company the way they do. The main one is that they are mentally taxing for customers. Clearly, simply clicking on the number of stars you want to give is less effortful than writing the review we just saw. Because of this, open-ended answers customers give are often very short, like "Good quality". In addition, without prompts to guide them, customers might forget to mention an important point.

There are ways in which you can mitigate this. The first one is relatively simple – in an online survey, the size of the field you leave for people to type in their response gives them an indication of what's expected of them. Make it (relatively) large so customers can think that you expect a long response. Adding an instruction to the question asking people for examples and details is also a common practice. In telephone interviews, the length of the customer's answer largely depends on how well the interviewer is leading the interview; if they are good and have established rapport with the customer, they will be able to get a high-quality answer.

Lastly, in recent years, vendors of customer experience measurement and management platforms have become truly ingenious in offering solutions for this issue. For example, when answering a study designed with InMoment, you would encounter their "AI-powered Engagement Engine™ [which] encourages rich conversations by listening and responding to customers in real-time, eliciting valuable responses" (InMoment, Active Listening Studio. Control the way you listen). The algorithm reads what you type in real-time and indicates the level of details you have provided in your answer; the result is updated constantly and shown to you on the screen.

A Close-Ended Question

I'd advise you whenever you can to follow up on the open-ended question with a close-ended one. "Whenever you can", in this case, means only one thing – when you think that questionnaire length will remain reasonable for the data collection method you've chosen and the customer's situation.

Such a question can take many forms. The simplest one is to ask customers, "What is the main reason you evaluate us like this?" and give them a list of options to choose from. A slightly more sophisticated version of the same question is to give customers the option to select multiple answers. I'm personally in favor of a third type of question (known as a grid question) in which customers are asked to share their views on several items by rating the company on a scale, say a 5- or a 7-point one.

There are two important disadvantages to these types of questions. The first one is that they take quite a bit of time to answer, so keep the list of items short; I've seen and done surveys with more than 20 items included here, and if I'm honest, even I find it tedious to answer to such questions. By keeping the list short, you stumble on the second disadvantage of these questions – the items you would include will often be quite generic, such as the ones I included in the example. These questions provide almost no detail. What if I answer that the quality is Excellent or Poor? Does this give the company enough to go on and implement improvements? Not at all.

What these questions give is guidance for further investigation. In a later chapter, we'll discuss the ways to analyze customer feedback. Still, it's worth mentioning here. Statistically speaking, by using a longer scale, these questions allow you to do more robust analytics. With an open-ended question, you would end up with a Yes/No answer; whether the customer spoke about quality or not, and whether they spoke of it positively or not. Such dichotomous variables are not ideal for statistical analysis. Longer scales, such as the 7-pt one in the example, do a better job of allowing more variability of responses.

A second reason to include such a close-ended question is that it prompts customers to give feedback on things they might have forgotten to mention in the open-ended question. On the latter, you would typically get the burning issues, such as what is on the forefront of the customers' mind, and that is important. But you would also like to get their opinion on other topics, like whether they like your product return policy or find the support you give them in creating value enough. I'm quite certain that only a few customers will mention these in an open-ended question, so if you want to know what people think, you'd have to ask them directly.

Both open- and close-ended questions are important in a customer feedback questionnaire. An important consideration is the length of the questionnaire.

Questionnaire Length

I've rarely seen consensus in the business world, such as questionnaire length. This is perhaps because all of us have had the chance to reply to surveys and we know this could be, well, why hide it – boring. Keeping your questionnaire short is the mantra here. Up to five minutes is ideal; up to 10 is acceptable in most cases. Longer surveys are inadvisable as respondents get tired and data quality is more difficult to maintain, not to mention that some will simply stop replying, further lowering the already low response rates.

Let's face it, this survey is important for you, but only rarely for your customer. You are collecting their feedback to do things better, and it's often not immediately clear to customers what exactly they get out of it. You would be doing everyone a favor if you keep the effort required by customers to a minimum, hence the advice to keep the questionnaire short.

This poses an important issue, though – how much insights can you get out of just a couple of questions? The answer that you don't want to hear, and I don't want to give, is "It depends". If you've already done several investigations before and you are using the study to monitor the development of customers' opinions, then you can get a lot out of it. In this situation, you would be looking for an overview of where you stand and whether you are moving the needle in the right direction. However, if you are looking for depth, you would have to supplement this survey with other sources of information. At the beginning of understanding customer needs, qualitative research can do miracles. Allowing for a much more in-depth investigation can serve as a great starting point for subsequent measurements. In addition, you can also run longer surveys; I advised you against it, and I still do but don't shy away from it too much. After all, if it needs to be done, it needs to be done. You can also get valuable insights by reading what people say about you on social media and customer reviews. These will also tremendously enrich what you know about customers' opinions and needs. Use what you already collect as well – your contact center most likely has a way of tracking what people are calling to complain about or ask, so you can also use this to broaden your view.

Later, we will discuss how to use all of these to gain a deeper understanding of your customer needs. For the time being, and to enable you to predict customer behavior, all you need is a short, concise questionnaire.

References

InMoment. Active listening studio. Control the way you listen. Retrieved from https://inmoment.com/active-listening-studio/#main

Middleton, F. (2019). Reliability vs validity in research | Differences, types and examples. Retrieved from www.scribbr.com/methodology/reliability-vs-validity/

Rise of the customer experience leader (2020 research report). Retrieved from www.mycustomer.com/resources/rise-of-the-customer-experience-leader-2020-research-report

7 Roadmap Step 3 – Input

Collect Customer Data

In a perfect world, at this point, you have a roadmap in place for designing and implementing a proactive personalized post-sales service (PPPS) program, you have the support of the people its execution depends on, and you have collected valid and reliable customer feedback. This is excellent news, as it means that you have half of the foundation of PPPS in place. It's now time to talk about the second half of the PPPS foundation – customer data.

What Is the Purpose of This Stage?

At the core of PPPS lies your ability to predict customer satisfaction on an individual customer level and act to contribute to creating value. You need three elements to do the first part – customer feedback, customer data, and state-of-the-art analytics. The purpose of this stage of your PPPS journey is to prepare the second of these pieces – customer data. There are five broad arrays of data that you might be interested in at this stage: usage data, interaction data, operational data, external data, and customer background data.

Types of Customer Data

Usage Data

Usage data encompasses all aspects of how the customer uses the product or the service, i.e., what do they do with it once they have it in place. Clearly, what this includes is vastly different from one industry to the next. To simplify things, we can think of usage data as described by two questions: when is the customer using the product, where, and what volume of it.

In telecommunications, for example, usage data for TV might include the frequency of watching TV and the TV channels watched. These could be related to frequency of driving, typical distance driven, and routes taken in the automotive sector. And in banking, you could see how often a customer is using their credit card, how big their purchases are, and where they are using it.

As you can see, there isn't an unlimited set of indicators of usage that can be utilized. The wealth and benefit of this kind of data come from the

DOI: 10.4324/9781003309284-10

fact that ideally, you would be able to track it in real-time and in very short intervals. For example, suppose you have minute-by-minute information on the frequency of watching TV. In that case, you can now create a plethora of other meaningful data points, like frequency of watching during a business day vs. a holiday and early in the day vs. in the evening. Additionally, you can also split all of this by channel watched.

Interaction Data

The second type of customer data you might want to collect is interaction data. In a nutshell, every time you and a customer are in touch directly, this creates interaction data.[1] This includes both the company-initiated and customer-initiated contact. Examples of the former would be every time you send customers newsletters or give them a call to present your latest proposition, sending them a proposal, or sending an invoice. Examples of customer-initiated contact are calls to your contact center, website visits, filing complaints, visiting a company's office, sending a request for an offer, or paying a bill.

In many ways, interaction data is much richer and complex than usage data, simply because there are many ways in which you can get in touch with customers. Interaction data is also more difficult to collect. If usage data is simply tracked, interaction data often needs to be created by you, as when a customer calls their account manager to ask for a proposal. The account manager's responsibility is to log this into the system you are using to monitor interaction data. We all share the experience that this is not a particularly reliable way of doing it. We'll talk more about this in the second part of this chapter.

Operational Data

This is perhaps the customer data area that companies are most capable of and used to collect. Operational data is concerned with what happens behind the scenes when a customer uses your product or service or when they interact with you. In the telecommunications example, this would be all the information about your network – throughput, bandwidth, etc. In the automotive example, all information about the condition of the various elements of your car is operational data. In short, this includes all indications of the workings of your company, product, or service when a customer applies pressure.

Note that whenever you make changes to your product or service, it is best to include it in this data set. For example, changing the supplier of alternators for the car you are manufacturing should be recorded in the data. Same with the software – when you update your product's software, say, smartwatch, make sure to note this, including the features you are updating. This will come in very handy when you run analytics to see how you can impact the customer value-creation process.

External Data

External data is all information that impacts and is relevant to the customer value-creation process and how your company supports it. Think about three streams of data here.

One would be related to your competitors, direct or otherwise. Whenever a competitor launches a new proposition, changes their pricing, or launches a sales campaign, this should create a data point in your data set.

The second aspect of external data that can be valuable in analyzing customer behavior is market regulations. Whenever a new regulation comes into effect, it is wise to add it as a data point in your data set to see its impact later on.

The third stream of external data concerns the context in which your product or service is being used. For example, weather or traffic conditions would be valuable for an automotive manufacturer, and the inflation rate could be important for a bank.

Customer Background Data

Customer background data, especially in its basic form, is available to virtually all companies. For example, this includes demographic variables to build a customer profile, like age, gender, region, etc. But don't limit yourself to demographics. Add information about the products and services the customer has purchased from you in the past, for example, bill size or any other relevant variables to describe the customer and the type of engagement you have with them.

Criteria for Success

So how do you know that you have enough of these data types to start predicting customer satisfaction? How do you know you have a good foundation to run predictive analytics?

Two of the criteria we discussed in the previous chapter also apply here. Your data must be valid and reliable. With customer feedback, validity is, in a sense, the bigger issue; with customer data, reliability is often the more difficult challenge.

Validity is less of an issue with customer data because you get what you measure directly. That is, if the sensors monitoring your network data, for example, or if your employees are honest and only record what they've actually done in a customer relationship management (CRM) system, whether the data is accurate isn't a major question.

However, what is often the case is that data is incomplete, especially when it requires human input. I'm not saying that you need to measure every bit of indicator that the parts in your car can produce; neither should you collect all possible customer background information, for example. Yet, in my experience, collecting interaction data, for example, can be a challenge, for it typically requires that an account manager or a salesperson fill this information in. Similarly, it is quite easy to neglect including external data or miss bits and pieces of it.

A third criterion for the quality of customer data you are collecting is whether it is up to date and reflects the latest movements on the indicators you are monitoring. Clearly, some pieces need to be updated only once in a while or on an as-needed basis. Things like customer background information or external data for competitors or regulations fall in this category. With the right systems in place, these pose no issue. Other indicators, such as usage or operational data, require much more frequent updates – ideally, you would have a real-time update on those.

The fourth and vital element you need to ensure is in place after you have completed this stage is whether all of these pieces of data – feedback, usage, and so on – can be connected. That is, do you have a full picture of individual customers' opinions and actions. From an execution perspective, this doesn't pose a considerable challenge. If you have a unique identifier for every customer and if it is present in every data set that you have, you can put it all together. From what I'm seeing in practice and reading about, fusing the data can often be a much bigger challenge than getting the data in the first place. Creating a common data set is more of an organizational and political challenge.

There are, I believe, two major requirements, the legal perspective aside, to meet when we talk about fusing all data pieces. They seem odd to point out, but I've seen them in practice, so it's worth talking about them.

Having common customer data set that people who are supposed to use it can get access to doesn't make sense. I've seen practically endless discussions between teams about who should have access to what, when, and under what conditions. While it can be risky to give everyone access to the data lake, going in the exact opposite direction and keeping it under lock is also not a very effective policy. A good process of governing data access is one way of solving this, and we'll cover that in the second half of this chapter.

The second requirement when discussing fusing customer feedback and customer data together, or to put it more mildly – a recommended condition – is to have one such data set. I'm flagging this as it is not uncommon for companies to maintain multiple versions of the same data; I've worked with companies who have told me that they have no less than five customer data sets in place. Five!

Summing it up, after this stage of the PPPS journey, you would have gathered or started gathering a host of customer data – usage, interaction, operational, external, and background one – and you would make it accessible (following clear rules) via a single data set linking the various data types. Next, we turn to a discussion of the best practices for achieving this.

Practical Advice on Collecting Customer Data

In their brilliant, and I feel underappreciated book, 'The Ends Game,' Marco Bertini and Oded Koenigsberg argued that a "company could be compensated for the quality of the outcomes it delivers, rather than the products and services it brings to market…" (Bertini & Koenigsberg, 2020, 1) One of the challenges in transitioning from a revenue model based on products or services to one based on value is how exactly the latter is done. Bertini and Koenigsberg tell the story of the comedy theater Teatreneu in Barcelona that solved this challenge with an ingenious solution called Pay Per Laugh. Entrance to shows is free – spectators pay absolutely nothing. Instead, Teatreneu charges customers for how many times they laugh during the show. They achieved this by making use of a "…facial recognition system mounted on the back of the seat in front of them…" (Bertini & Koenigsberg, 2020, 77). One laughter costs 30 Euro cents, and there is a cap on the maximum amount a customer could pay at 24 Euro (80 laughs).

What I love about this story is how well it exemplifies how technology can fundamentally alter how we think about data collection. Just ten years ago, to get this kind of information, you would probably have to interview customers exiting the show and ask them how many times they laughed: an unreliable measure if there was any.

These days, most of the data types we discussed earlier are easy to obtain. Customer background data should be a non-issue for any company that deals directly with customers – it has become commonplace, especially with the advent of e-commerce, to register when making purchases. Before that, many customers' information was available in contracts and other purchase documents. It's a matter of storing this information appropriately rather than collecting it differently.

Operational data is also largely available. Production monitoring technologies have been available for decades, and they have been becoming more detailed and accurate as time goes on. Besides having direct access to the products, companies can get a lot of this data by testing the products in their development labs.

External data related to regulations is available freely and to all players in the market. Competitive intelligence might be more difficult to obtain, but it's becoming easier to get to know what your competitors are up to with the internet. Of course, you probably wouldn't have information about the internal workings of your competitors, but that's not a must to run a successful PPPS program. Finally, information about the customers' context in terms of bigger societal and economic trends is also available freely, and it's a matter of choosing the relevant pieces rather than anything else.

We already touched upon the key difficulty with collecting interaction data – the fact that if it requires human input, it might be less reliable, as people might simply forget to add it to your system. The basic solutions for this, I believe, are automation, simplification, and motivation. Nowadays, most CRM systems used for gathering interaction data can automate the process. For example, they can automatically add emails sent between account managers and customers to your interactions database; contact center data has been gathered this way for decades. What also helps in the process is to make it very easy for people to add the information to your CRM – add-ons available for email clients, for example, make it easier for account managers to fill it in the system. Often, things come down to the old but gold human motivation. Explaining to account managers why this information is important and including it as a job requirement would be two simple steps you can take to increase the CRM fill-in rate. At the end of the day, if you are in touch with the customer, someone in your organization knows about it – it's a matter of recording this information.

Finally, usage data might represent a bigger challenge in some industries, depending on the capacity for connectivity that's put into the products or services. In some sectors, it's relatively easy to monitor usage. Internet providers, for example, have absolutely no issue with that. It's also easy to monitor credit card usage simply because the transactions happen via connected devices (POS terminals). Things might get much trickier if we talk about consumer electronics, for example. Traditional products like non-connected LED bulbs or hair dryers have no way of collecting or sharing usage data back with you. Yet, the smartification these industries are undergoing makes it viable to obtain usage data because of the sensors embedded in these devices. For example, many smart lighting products are controlled by customers via the internet, which means that they can also send back usage data. The same goes for cars, cameras, and smartwatches. Of course, you need to ensure that you have the right to collect this data, which depends on the market regulations in place. Typically, customer consent ensures that you can lawfully gather and use it, but there might be trickier cases for which I advise you to consult with your legal department.

Now that you have all this data, it's important that you tie it together. An Aberdeen Group study (Lock, 2017) on the use of data lakes and the conditions that enable it highlights one aspect of this that we discussed briefly earlier – connecting all the data is not so much a technological, but rather an organizational and often political challenge. The leaders in data-lake usage have a better process supporting data sharing across functions (process). They encourage data-driven decisions (culture); they have a formal way of supporting users to connect new data sources (process), and they upskill their personnel (training and development). This is also echoed by McKinsey, who claim that "…the most successful early adopters are designing their data lakes using a 'business back' approach, rather than considering technology factors first" (McKinsey, 2017).

In practice, it is a good idea to start by writing down the answers to a handful of questions like Who will be using the data? How are you going to get the data in? And perhaps most insightfully, "How are you going to protect the data in your repository and ensure it's of good quality while still making it available for everyone?" (Talend) These answers will guide your design of an organizational structure and process to kick start the process. Sol Rashidi, Chief Analytics Officer at The Estee Lauder Companies says, "Know what data matters most, prioritize it, build the discipline to protect and govern it, then democratize the data to enable your data specialists and end-users to extract the insights they need to innovate" (MIT Technology

Review Insights). In a single sentence, Rashidi touches on a lot of the vital elements for data management we discussed. Particularly insightful, I believe, is the democratization of data. You can no longer keep it locked somewhere; this is not your private lake. True, there should be some restrictions to its use. However, democracy also doesn't mean anarchy – it's about the rules that you put in place that allow a vast number of people to use it without breaking the system.

What I believe you will also benefit from is once you have started to put all the data together, write down all of the answers you come up with on the fly, i.e., turn them into organizational processes. The goal is not to become a rigid bureaucratic organization, of course, but rather to ensure stability in the way your data management team operates. The way to avoid political disputes within the organization is to try and govern them preemptively.

The creation of one data set which includes all the information you have gathered about customers – feedback, usage, interaction, operational, external, and background data – marks an important milestone in your PPPS journey. You now have all the prerequisites to start running analytics to predict customer behavior, so you can be proactive and offer personalized post-sales service to your full customer base. There is a plan, there is buy-in, and there is data in place. Next, we will start analyzing this data!

Note

1 I'm deliberately pointing toward 'direct' contact, to distinguish it from the fact that when a customer uses their product, they are also interacting with you – after all it's your company's product or service, so they are in touch with you. When I use 'interaction data' in the book, what I have in mind is this direct contact.

References

Bertini, M., & Koenigsberg, O. (2020). *The Ends Game: How Smart Companies Stop Selling Products and Start Delivering Value (Management on the Cutting Edge)*. Kindle Edition. MIT Press.

Lock, M. (2017). Angling for insight in today's data lake, angling for insight in today's Data Lake. Retrieved from ibm.com

McKinsey. (2017). Digital, A smarter way to jump into data lakes. Retrieved from www.mckinsey.com/business-functions/mckinsey-digital/our-insights/a-smarter-way-to-jump-into-data-lakes

MIT Technology Review Insights. Building a high-performance data and AI organization. Retrieved from https://mittrinsights.s3.amazonaws.com/HighPerformanceAI.pdf

Talend. Definitive guide to cloud data warehouses and cloud data lakes. Retrieved from www.talend.com/resources/definitive-guide-cloud-data-warehouses/

8   Roadmap Step 4 – Understanding

Analyze the Data

What Is the Purpose of This Stage?

Ideally, at this point, you have a valid and reliable view of what your customers think about your products and services and about the things they do in the wild. This is still nothing more than a huge pile of data – you only have the bricks in place. On the other hand, nothing was ever built without physical materials, has it? It is time that we start working with your data.

The essence of customer analytics, and in fact of any analytical process, is to answer two questions: what is happening (descriptive analytics) and why (diagnostic analytics). Both of these serve the one question that we suggested earlier: the never-ending dream of humanity – how to influence what's happening and what will happen if I try to do it in this particular way.

For now, we don't need to worry about the latter two questions – they will become relevant at the next stage when you start acting to influence the value-creation process. Our purpose at this stage of the proactive personalized post-sales service (PPPS) journey is to understand what people think of your product or service and why they think it. In an ideal world, after this has been completed, you would have a clear overview of the extent to which your customers think you are supporting them enough in their value-creation process and the reasons they think so.

Answering what is happening? is a fairly easy part of the process. Everything known as descriptive analytics helps address this question. Put simplistically, even if you only use the key performance indicator (KPI) you chose when you gathered customer feedback, it might be a good enough foundation. You want to know what's the temperature, what's the lay of the land. Are we, as a company, giving our customers enough so they can create value for themselves? This is implicit in the most popular metrics, such as Net Promoter Score (NPS) and overall satisfaction; they are both going to give you a good indication of where you stand. Of course, don't forget to look at the overall result and within specific customer groups, say, your target personas. But we are getting ahead of ourselves – more on this in the second half of this chapter.

The answer to Why? It poses a lot more difficulties, and in my humble view, we, myself included, often ask it in an unstructured manner. I've come

DOI: 10.4324/9781003309284-11

to believe that there are many different senses in which the Why? questions are asked, and these need to be distinguished as they lead to different answers. Let's see this in an example.

Imagine that you understand that 'what is happening' is that your customers are not happy with your product or service – they are not creating enough value with it. If you are like me, you'd immediately ask yourself why they think so. This is the first sense in which the Why? question exists – why someone thinks so. For this exercise, let's assume that the answer is something along the lines of "The product or service is not reliable enough". From here, we've got at least three different options:

- We can continue the same chain and ask, "And why do customers think the product or service is unreliable?" We might come to understand, for example, that they've experienced two internet outages in the last two months, or that their car breaks down too often, or that their payments do not go through on time. Clearly, there are subtle differences between these answers, so you've got an insight. In customers' terms, reliability might mean whether something is happening or not (internet outage vs. no internet outage) or speed (the payment is going through, just slowly). At this point, you might want to revisit your 'what is happening' answer and see if it needs adjustment.

- The second 'why' you can ask, knowing that customers deem your product or service unreliable, is why they want it to be reliable? Why is this an important criterion? If the first option puts us down the path of understanding the specific reasons behind the evaluation, this second option is more concerned with what people want from the product or service and what they value. For some products or services, the answer will be quite clear at first. Take home internet as an example. The question, 'why people want reliable home internet?' might even seem slightly ridiculous at first. However, I still encourage you to ask it because you might end up with very interesting findings that impact how you act later. Could it be that they need reliability because their kids are watching YouTube? Or because they are in 8 hours straight online calls? Or because they are mining bitcoins? Quite different applications of the same product, as we can see, and maybe, there are different ways for you to solve the issue knowing what value customers are creating with the product.

- The third sense of asking 'Why' is more related to you than to the customer and concerns what you did, leading to product or service unreliability. Is your network not strong enough? Did you experience too much traffic on Monday morning? Was there a glitch in your car parts supply leading you to use substandard parts? Was it something you did when the customer called the contact center?

As you can see, there are many ways of asking 'Why' that enrich our understanding of the issue at hand; none of them is useless. Yet, they lead in substantially different directions. I believe any analytical exercise should include an investigation in all three directions – why they say it, why they want it, and why it happened. The first helps you pinpoint the exact root cause; the second gives you a more holistic view of the customer-as-a-person; the third links it back to your actions.

In my experience, these are the questions that you need to have answered. After having a good read on what's going on, the outcomes that you should aim for are: How well are you currently contributing to the customers' value-creation process? Also, the answer to the multiple aspects of why is this the current state of affairs. Why do customers think what they think? Why do they want what they want? And why did they end up with this evaluation of your products or services (i.e., what is it that you did to drive it)?

You will probably not achieve this by running a single study; in all likelihood, you'll need a whole analytical program to answer these questions, and I strongly urge you to consider multiple points of view and sources of insights. 'What are the things you can do?' is the topic of the second part of this chapter.

Practical Advice on Running Customer Analytics

My recommendation for running analytics that will lead to taking actions to contribute more to the customer value-creation process is to describe what is going on and then look for the causal relationships between the elements of the customer experience. Look for the root causes of dissatisfaction or suboptimal value-creation.[1] The first part helps to think of this exercise as a conversation with a stranger that you want to know well. Ask many questions that will help you get acquainted with this person. Who is he? What does he think of us? Where does he like going? How often does he use our product or service? There are no right or wrong questions. For the second part, understanding the causal relationships between things, you'll go deeper and look for the reasons why; I like to imagine this as a more intimate conversation where we try to understand why this person is the way he is.

Descriptive Stage

Customer Feedback

The first step in the analytical stage, from my perspective, is to understand where you stand in terms of customer feedback – are your customers happy with what you are providing? Start with the KPI you have chosen to use earlier in the process, during the customer feedback collection. If it's NPS, calculate NPS; if it's overall satisfaction, calculate the average result or the share of people who are very or at least partially satisfied.

Next, what I like to do is to look at the KPI result by customer groups. These could be the traditional, rather simply defined groups, like age, gender, region, location, etc. When I say, 'simply defined,' I don't mean that this is useless. Quite the contrary, it can be a very beneficial exercise, as it helps you focus your further investigations. For example, if it turns out that people in one particular city are unhappy with your network coverage, that already gives you enough to dig deeper. Or, if a specific age group is less happy with your credit card service than the others, it makes perfect sense to understand more about this group's specific experience.

All of this can be done with the data you already have at hand. In addition, you might want to consider running a competitive benchmarking exercise, either via a quantitative survey or by using social media analytics. A competitive benchmarking will tell you where you stand compared to the competitors. It is unlikely that such a study will be helpful on its own, but it can give you two things. On the one hand, if you know that you are doing much worse than your competitors, this could create a sense of urgency within the organization. And even if you are the leader, you can still pinpoint areas in which the competitors might attack you in the future or practices you can adopt from them.

To get a competitive view of customer feedback, you can also look at the ratings customers post on retailers' websites, such as Amazon. With thousands of ratings, these are quickly becoming retail channels and an important source of insights. There are two benefits to doing this, in addition to knowing where you stand vs. the competitors. On the one hand, this is probably the only source of information that can give you insights on the stock keeping unit (SKU) level. Even with the best intention, it's close to impossible to achieve this in a survey; for example, one reason is that if you have a lot of SKUs, you are going to need a huge sample size. On the other hand, what you see on retailers' websites is also what customers see there, which makes it a great way to put yourself in your customers' shoes.

When you are finished with this stage, you will have a pulse check. Are we in trouble or not? Are there pockets of customers at risk of churning because they are unhappy or not? Are there groups of customers we are not fully supporting in their value-creation efforts?

Usage Data

Next to descriptive analytics on customer feedback, you might want to run them on the usage data you've gathered as well. As a reminder, you are looking to get to know your customers and not to look for the reasons for high or low usage of your product or service – this we'll do later. Explore the types of customers you have and the usage patterns of your product or services. Do you see customers who use their credit cards mostly over the weekend and for relatively large purchases? Do you see customers who use their smartphones to upload many videos? Do you see customers who regularly drive their cars on short trips outside of the city? The only limits to the questions you can ask here are the ones set by your imagination.

Ethnographic research, or the practice to "visit consumers in their homes or offices to observe and listen in a nondirected way" (Anderson, 2009), can also be valuable to understand how your customers use your product or service. David Burrows gives an excellent example of a company using ethnographic research:

> German household goods manufacturer Miele, for example, observed constant cleaning in homes where some family members were suffering from allergies. As a result, it designed a vacuum cleaner with a traffic light indicator that shows when a surface is dust-free"
>
> (Burrows, 2014)

Olaf Dietrich of Miele, explains: "…we realize that it is essential for not only marketing but also engineers to see the issues first-hand. Only if you are present do you really understand the issues" (Burrows, 2014). And the issues, I want to add, that are related to value-creation.

A second example of using ethnographic research to understand customer needs and embed a solution in products and services comes from HTC. Their work

> has led to some of the new functions on its HTC One (M8) phone: the 'motion launch' function – the ability to lock and unlock the device with a double-tap on the screen, and the auto-answer, by which calls are answered when the phone is lifted to the ear.
>
> (Burrows, 2014)

In both cases, the insights that led to product improvements were unlocked by carefully and methodically observing what people do with the product.

Interaction Data

This would be known as customer journey mapping to those of you in the marketing or CX fields. This part of the analytics is to understand what customers are going through as they interact with your company. What is the sequence of events that unfolds? Do they first go to your website to search for support and then reach out to your contact center? How soon after? Which sections of your website do they visit? Do they go to your office to look for help? Have they had to return your product for some reason? At the end of the day, you will have a journey-looking map of the interactions between customers and you. There is probably no need to say it, but this will be extremely valuable when you design your actions, as it will give you a good view of the touchpoints you have with customers.

The latter is especially valid if you are measuring touchpoint satisfaction, as most leaders in customer experience do. In addition to an overall KPI for the company, product, or service, many companies employ touchpoint measurement to monitor customers' evaluations on the same indicator for each interaction they have with the company. This helps a lot in targeting your efforts, and I strongly recommend implementing such a practice.

Operational Data

Most of the key players in every industry I know would constantly monitor how their products or services are working, and they use it actively to improve the efficiency of their operations. Have a look at whatever is relevant for your own business. In services, for example, these could be things like service times – how long does it take you to serve a customer; does it differ by time of day; is it consistent in time? Or, if you are manufacturing a product, have a look at its respective operational KPIs.

External Data

Like other data types, it's worth looking at what's happening in the wider context, beyond the interaction between your company and the customer. This would include, for example, product launches by competitors and their promotional campaigns, changes in the regulatory framework, major trends in customer behavior, and even contextual factors like weather, inflation rate, market growth, etc. Simply looking at these can give you important insights into where the market is headed, and more importantly, where people's lives are headed.

Customer Background Information

What we said in the beginning of this section about descriptive analytics being a lot like getting to know a person is perhaps best exemplified by this kind of analytics run on customer background information. Look for everything you can get your hands on about your customers. Contract length, changes in usage plans, number of times they've paid their bills on time, marital status – whatever you can think of.

It is often difficult to obtain that kind of data simply because you can't ask customers everything. There are analytical ways to circumvent this. A leading consumer electronics company, a client of the company I work for, was trying to enrich their customers' information in their customer relationship management (CRM) system by adding, for example, education level, income, and other variables. The issue most B2B2C companies face is that they don't have direct access to customers, so they can't ask them for this information. Although a lot of customer background information is publicly available, the difficulty lies in the fact that it is available in an aggregated level, for example, on a postal code one. We designed and implemented a micro segmentation to link the two, allowing us to append the CRM data with the publicly available one on the customer level. We started by creating hundreds of segments from their CRM system, and then had a look at these same segments on postal code level. At the second stage, we supplemented the CRM system with the additional information available for each segment on postal code level. The downside of this approach is that it can only provide a proxy – every customer in the same segment in the CRM received the same value for personal income and education level, for example. As with any estimations, this is not a perfect solution, but it is a viable one.

Have a Look at Cross-Sections of Data

One of the most valuable things about having a customer data lake is the opportunity to dig deeper, for example, by looking at different pieces of data in conjunction. Explore, for example, how customer satisfaction changes with customer service time. How does your product behave when used more than usual? How do long-term customers use your product compared to new users? Do customers contact your contact center more immediately after buying a product or sign up for a service? The variety of questions you can ask is immense, just like the value you can get out of these types of analytics. To explore is the best recommendation I can give you for this. The benefit lies in finding a hidden nugget of gold, and for that, one needs to go through a mass of earth.

Now that you have a clear view of where you stand on each of these aspects, it's time to move to the core part of the analytical stage and figure out why is all of this happening.

Diagnostic Stage

This, together with taking the actions to increase your contribution to the customers' value-creation process, is perhaps the most important stage of the PPPS journey. We are looking to understand the reasons behind customers' evaluation of your company or its product or service. We aim for three things: depth, detail, and linkage to things you can act on.

Customer Research

A good place to start the investigation is to look at the customer feedback survey results alone. Remember that we included two questions as a follow-up to your KPI – one of them was open-ended, and the other asked for customers' evaluations on several pre-defined criteria. Both will come in handy here.

As a first step, look at what customers say drives their evaluation when you ask them about it. Nowadays, dozens of text analytics platforms can parse, after setting them up, huge volumes of text and summarize it for you. The insights you gain from this exercise can prove invaluable for understanding customer satisfaction or dissatisfaction. A great example of this comes from one of the leading sports apparel brands. One of their more successful stores closed down for a renovation in the spring of 2019, and after it reopened, its sales were significantly lower than before. Naturally, this begs the question why. Luckily, our client has a very good customer experience measurement program. They collect customer feedback via tablets at the stores' exit; they ask customers to provide an open comment. We started digging into what customers were saying in their words. We discovered that a sizable number of customers were complaining about the curtains' length in the dressing rooms, which were indeed shorter than before. This made them uncomfortable trying many things at the store, leading to lower sales. I have been in the market research business for over 15 years, and I think I'm doing a decent job. Yet, it would have never occurred to me to ask about the length of the curtains in a quantitative survey – this insight was only made possible by looking at what people share with us in their words.

Further to analyzing the feedback customers provide, you can understand the importance of certain aspects of the product or the service to customers by looking at the close-ended question we added to the feedback survey. If the open-ended question gives you what is known in the industry as stated importance, i.e., what customers claim is important to them, the close-ended one allows you to find out the so-called derived importance. Open-ended questions, in my view, are a fantastic tool for gauging customers' opinions. However, they suffer from one major flaw – very often, when asked why they are unhappy, people often say things like Price or Quality. How generic this is aside, these answers hide the fact that people must make trade-offs in real life. In a perfect world, free BMWs would be the norm. As we don't live in this world (yet), we must make sacrifices when we make decisions. Derived importance helps us achieve that. Its essence lies in statistically estimating the strength of the relationship between certain elements, say, customers' evaluation of price and your overall KPI, or the evaluation of your contact center and your KPI. What you get out of this is a view of which aspect drives customers' overall evaluation, and you get it in a non-biased manner. In essence, you are linking two otherwise separate things to develop a more realistic view.

One other way of figuring out the 'why' behind customers' evaluations is to conduct qualitative research, in pretty much any of its many forms, depending on what fits best with your goals and industry. In-depth interviews and focus group discussions are the two most widely used methods, but there are others, such as ethnographic research, which we discussed before. Unlike quantitative research, these allow for much more probing, hence also a depth of insights; one drawback of qualitative research is that it doesn't allow you to come up with a numerical expression of your findings, which I've found puts people off sometimes. In my view, there is no need for this to be the case, as numbers are not always the be-all-end-all of analyses. The opportunity to hear people telling stories and anecdotes related to your company and its products and services is priceless, and I'd recommend that you don't miss it.

Speaking about depth, I'd like to mention one other source of information. Earlier, we mentioned that one way of benchmarking yourself against your competitors is to look at the customers' ratings on retailers' websites and webpages. In addition to this, you can also look at the customers' reviews. A good part of them is so detailed and insightful that they are akin to conducting qualitative research. The benefit is that the findings could potentially be translated to numbers. Analyzing user-generated content in any form is similar to conducting qualitative research at scale, which is a recipe for success.

If there is one common drawback of all these ways of understanding why people evaluate you the way they do, they can't directly answer the third sense in which we asked the 'why' question. Everything so far can give you an idea of why people say what they do and why they want what they want. The major issue in the analytics and insights industry, which I've heard repeated thousands of times, is linking these answers to your actions, i.e., answering the third why. I think that this is behind the fair demand from research and analytics users for suppliers to give them actionable insights. Ultimately, you know how customers feel and think. Unfortunately, that's not worth a penny if you can't influence it.

Before the boom in data availability, companies used to solve this in a good old-fashioned way – self-reflection. I have sat with dozens of clients in long workshops where we try to figure out what they are doing behind customers' evaluations, and I loved every second of it. But the thing is, these exercises are very dependent on one crucial element – people willing to participate in discovering what is very often issues in the way they do things. This level of open-mindedness, which is often coupled with a culture con-ducive to openly sharing feedback, is unfortunately not something you can easily get or create everywhere. Often, people tend to get protective and argue that the analytics are wrong, rather than there might be areas for improvement in how they do things. Spurring action becomes an endless game of pushing and pulling, which is more often than I'd like to admit a futile exercise. In a word, many companies fail to act on customer feedback and analytics because the latter are often generic and not directly linked to their actions.

Linking KPIs to Interaction and Operational Data

There is a fundamental shift in our ability to understand the why behind customers' evaluations. It is driven by the expansion of data availability, and artificial intelligence (AI) looks for answers across data sources. While not perfect and not fully solving the action question, this kind of analysis brings us many steps forward to action. Analytics becomes truly powerful when you can directly link your overall KPI, why people evaluate you this way, and your actions. This is what the customer data lake you created unlocks.

By now, you have the right foundation to do this. The ingredients are simple enough to write down: customer feedback fused in a common data set with customer data in its five forms (usage, interaction, operational, external, and customer background data). To get insights out of it, you get a good chef to stir it all together in a pot and cook it, i.e., apply top-notch data science capabilities to the pool of data you have.

The essence of the workflow you can use to understand how your interactions with customers impact their evaluation of your products or services is this:

- Get your overall KPI and the evaluations by items (i.e., satisfaction drivers)
- Get your interaction data next to the above
- Run analytics:
  - Prepare and run algorithms to understand how impactful each of the interaction elements is
  - Put the volume of people who go through each interaction for a certain amount of time next to the latter
  - Figure out how much it would cost you to fix this

We already spoke at length about the first two items on the list, so we'll focus a bit more on the analytics. I'm suggesting that you understand the impact of every interaction and prioritize improvements based on this impact and its size, i.e., how many customers have this experience in the first place. Neither of the two elements is enough on its own to give you a good view of where to focus, but in conjunction, they make obvious the areas where you can expect the highest return. Here's why.

The impact of each interaction will be a number that indicates how much it influences customers' overall opinion of your company (or its products or services). Based on this, you will know, for example, that a successful resolution after a single call to your contact center will have a very positive impact on your overall KPI. For example, a call to your contact center made after the customer has visited the frequently asked questions section on your website has a mildly negative impact. Also, a journey consisting of a website visit, a visit to your office, and a contact center call has a very negative impact. This begins to clarify things for you a bit. If your contact center does a good job providing a single-interaction resolution, customers will be happy with you. And if customers have to take a lengthier journey, they would be unhappy.

What you still need to add to the mix is how often each of these happens. For example, a single-call resolution will yield a positive result, but how often do you manage to do it? If it's only in 50% of the cases, and if 50% of your customers contact you over 6 months, this means that 25% of your customers never experience this, i.e., they take different journeys. Alternatively, it could be that just 2% of your customers have to take the lengthier journey (so 1% of all your customers). From this perspective, it might be better to focus on increasing the number of single-call resolutions rather than fixing your frequently asked questions. Then, people could find their answers there. Another option is to upskill your office personnel to provide good solutions, after which customers don't have to call your contact center.

I wish this was the end of the prioritization efforts, but it's not. A crucial element of the mix is figuring out the kind of investment you would need for this. Customers need to make trade-offs when choosing products or services to buy, and companies need to do the same. We might want to fix everything and live happily ever after, but the harsh reality is that there's always a price tag. We might be better off deciding not to fix something, as cynical as it may sound, especially if it wouldn't have a proportionate impact on your KPIs.

Next is running analytics to understand which journeys and which parts of the journey influence customers' overall evaluation. You can, especially if you have robust data, do the same with operational KPIs. Like all driver analyses we discussed in this chapter, this involves:

- Get your overall KPI and the evaluations by items (i.e., satisfaction drivers)
- Get your operational data next to the above
- Run analytics:
  - Prepare and run AI algorithms to understand how much each operational KPI impacts customer feedback
  - Put the volume of people who have experience with the products or services described by the operational KPIs
  - Figure out how much it would cost you to fix this
  - Additionally, you can also establish thresholds for operational KPI performance

As you can see, the logic is the same as running analytics with interaction data. First, understand which operational drivers impact customer feedback. For example, you can answer questions like how much upload internet speed impacts customers' evaluation, the influence of a single brief internet outage, or how a 10% drop in internet speed affects customers' evaluation. As a second step, you can look at how often these things happen. It might turn out that a 10% drop in internet speed often happens while brief outages are much rarer. Next, you'd have to make the same trade-off calculation – is it worth fixing each of these immediately, given the costs involved, or is there a workaround?

In addition, this analysis also allows you to set evidence-based thresholds for your operational KPIs. This allows you to set targets for your internal teams. If you know that an outage longer than 5 minutes causes a significant drop in customer feedback, you can set yourself the goal of not having more than five of these per year.

To be fair, the analytics we discussed in this chapter are merely scratching the surface of what's possible. I guess a data scientist could rightfully exclaim after Archimedes'[2] "give me enough data and access to it, and I shall move the world". With the amount and variety of data, and importantly – with the ability to connect otherwise disparate data points – you have this power in your hands. Knowing what your customers think of you and your products and services and linking it with different customer data unlocks previously unimaginably actionable analytics. Ideally, after this stage, you have a good view of customers' opinions and what's driving them, which are the critical ingredients for the next stage – taking action.

Notes

1 As we mentioned earlier, there are a number of ways to achieve these; for simplicity, I'll split each into two parts – things you can do with the data lake you already created, and additional elements you can add to the mix.
2 The original quote by Archimedes is "Give me a lever long enough and a fulcrum on which to place it, and I shall move the world".

References

Anderson, K. (2009). Ethnographic research: A key to strategy. *Harvard Business Review*. Retrieved from https://hbr.org/2009/03/ethnographic-research-a-key-to-strategy

Burrows, D. (2014). How to use ethnography for in-depth consumer insight. Retrieved from www.marketingweek.com/how-to-use-ethnography-for-in-depth-consumer-insight/

9 Roadmap Step 5 – Action

Initiatives for Customer Inspiration, Motivation, Education, and Adjustments on the Fly

What Is the Purpose of This Stage?

At this point, you have in your hands all the tools that you need to work and increase your contribution to customers' value-creation process or to remove barriers from that process, albeit still reactively – after all, we based everything we know on the portion of customers you cover with your customer feedback survey and those who complain. Nevertheless, you know where you stand currently and the weak points, i.e., which elements you might want to address. It's time to do it.

The purpose of this stage of the proactive personalized post-sales service (PPPS) design and implementation journey is two-fold. One, although you don't have a view of how each customer thinks, your customer feedback survey still covers, hopefully, a high enough number of them, i.e., you have enough on your hands to start making an impact. The first goal here is to act based on your feedback and improve things for those customers who share it. This is known as implementing a close-the-loop program, in which you collect feedback and act on it. These actions will then become a learning ground for the final elements of the PPPS program that we'll develop in the next chapter.

The second goal I'd like to propose that you set yourself is to test the effectiveness of your interventions before you scale them up at the next stage. The logic of PPPS is that you act proactively to address customers' needs, and you do it at scale. So far, we still haven't implemented the proactive and the scalability elements – this we will do at the next stage. But before you go big, I think it's worth testing if your solutions actually work. This is not unlike the journey start-ups go through. To get funding for their growth, they usually have to show a great idea and get some traction for it. Similarly, you want to know if there is evidence that what you do to boost customers' value-creation and remove barriers achieves these goals; you'd better do it on a smaller scale.

I suggest two criteria by which you can judge the success at this stage of the PPPS journey. The first one is related to culture and to the company's ability to get things done and is the answer to the question "Is the company taking action?", i.e., "Are we acting on the feedback customers share on individual customer level?" You can think of this as an expression of

DOI: 10.4324/9781003309284-12

how customer-centric and willing the organization is to contribute to the customers' value-creation process. It is difficult to recommend a threshold for this indicator. In a perfect world, you would want to react to 100% of the feedback you receive; after all, this is the reason you are gathering this feedback in the first place. Clearly, we don't live in a perfect world, so that's impossible to achieve. I'd aim for at least 80% coverage, especially among unhappy customers, and act within 48 to 72 hours from receiving the feedback. Neither of these is overwhelming with the right organizational structure, technology, and culture in place.

Getting a reading on the second criterion for the success of the action stage of your PPPS program is one of the biggest pain points for businesses of all shapes and sizes: "Is what we are doing working?", i.e., "What is the impact of our initiatives on CX and our financial metrics?" In a 2021 survey among over 1,000 customer experience (CX), marketing, and analytics professionals, Pointillist found that

> While organizations are measuring customer experience KPIs, they lack the means to connect these metrics to business outcomes. Almost half (41%) of companies say that they capture improvements in metrics like NPS® or customer satisfaction, but they are challenged to translate that into revenue or costs.
>
> (Ventura, 2021)

Also, in 2021, McKinsey reported that "Only 4% of CX leaders believe their CX measurement system enables them to calculate a decision's return on investment" (McKinsey & Company, 2021a).

This is a huge challenge for all CX practitioners. If we don't know whether what we are doing works or not, how do we know if we should do more of the same or completely change the course of action? How can we propel our organizations to act if we can't show that these actions are making a dent? After all, you and I probably wouldn't keep doing what we do in our daily lives if we don't see improvements, would we? Why would an organization be any different? Calculating the impact of our actions is neither optional nor a nice-to-have feature. In the years to come, the ability to track this would be a must for all companies willing to help their customers improve their well-being.

In summary, I recommend that you look for two things at this stage of your PPPS journey: establishing a culture and practices for acting on customer feedback and being able to monitor the impact of your actions on both customers' attitudes and your business results. How do you go about this?

Practical Advice on Kickstarting and Running Initiatives for Customer Inspiration, Motivation, Education, and Adjustments on the Fly

In my experience, four interrelated elements make a close-the-loop program a success: committing to it, the capability to generate actions, the technology to execute your program in a scalable fashion, and the ability to measure return on investment. Let's tackle them one by one.

Commitment

Very rarely are great initiatives executed by one person alone; cooperation is one of the defining characteristics of our species, and there's a good reason for that — together, we achieve much more. When it comes to running a successful close-the-loop program, there are (at least) two groups of stakeholders to consider.

As the program will require time and money, a good place to start is to get buy-in from the relevant stakeholders. We already touched upon this in a previous chapter, so we'll not dig deeper into it. Suffice it to say that getting buy-in from budget holders is akin to developing a business plan for a company. Having a personal, close relationship with them also helps, of course, and being a trusted partner in the business wouldn't hurt either. Yet, in my experience, no one can resist a well-thought-out thorough plan for improving business metrics like revenue or profit. Use whatever success stories from companies similar to yours you can get to showcase how others have done it, and if possible, invite them in the room to share their experience. Nothing works as well as hearing a success story from its source.

The second major group of people whose collaboration you'd need to develop an impactful close-the-loop program is the people who will make it a reality. These might be your colleagues in your contact center, CX champions, or customer care specialists. Whoever they are, you will need their commitment to making it a reality.

The framework I like to think about this through was initially developed by two psychologists, Martin Fishbein and Icek Ajzen, in the 1980s. After its latest update, it is called Theory of Planned Behavior. They propose that human behavior is driven by "three kinds of considerations: beliefs about the likely consequences of my behavior, beliefs about what important others think I should do, and beliefs about my ability to carry out the behavior" (Ajzen & Schmidt, 2020, 17).

That is, whether we'll do something or not depends on "the person's subjective probability that performing a behavior of interest will lead to a certain outcome (instrumental behavioral beliefs) or involve a certain experience (experiential behavioral beliefs)" (Ajzen & Schmidt, 2020, 20). In our case, whether your colleagues will close the loop with customers depend on whether they believe this will bring a certain outcome for them or the customer. The question we need to answer here to motivate them to act is, "whether closing-the-loop going to be beneficial for the customer, me, or for both of us, and in which way?" What will people achieve by performing this action?

The second element that helps people intend to do something is what others around us do or think. We can think of this as asking two closely related yet distinctive questions. First, "Will the people who are important to me approve or disapprove it if I act to close the loop?" The answer to this question highlights the importance of having support for your PPPS program from every layer of the organization. Due to the hierarchical structure of an organization, the top management's opinion will be valued the most. Therefore, it is important that they encourage this kind of behavior. The second question people ask themselves when engaging in new behaviors, consciously or not, is whether the people whose opinion is important to them do the same thing. This insight is behind the widely spread practice of giving examples and providing testimonials. They serve exactly the purpose of telling the audience, "Look, I'm like you, and I'm doing this". In addition, it also highlights the importance of getting a couple of active promoters of your program early on and making them successful. Nothing signals the appropriateness of behavior like seeing others being valued for doing it.

The third aspect that helps people form an intention to do something is the amount of control people think they have over the situation, i.e., the "person's subjective probability that a given facilitating or inhibiting factor will be present in the situation of interest" (Ajzen & Schmidt, 2020, 20). When people think they have the skills and knowledge to cope with a certain situation, they are more likely to engage in it. Translating it to the situation we are discussing in this book; if people believe they have what it takes to support customers' value-creation efforts, they will be more likely to act on this belief. Training people to acquire the needed skills and allowing them to share examples between themselves is vital. Both would make them more confident in their ability to do what's right, making it more likely that they'll commit to your program.

Now, these attitudes don't guarantee that people will start taking action, but they vastly increase the chances that they will. You can try it out yourself on a behavior you started (or stopped) recently. See if these elements were in place: Did you believe it will help you advance toward a certain goal? Did you see others doing it, or at the very least, do you think they approve of it? Did you think you could handle it? In the majority of cases, they will be there.

Technology

The second key consideration when designing your close-the-loop program is technology. You've probably noticed that I didn't talk about technology too much in this book. I didn't do it not because I don't think it's important; quite the contrary. I forbore an in-depth discussion as I risk going into almost advertisement mode on the one hand and the other, because I think it can often distract us from focusing on what we are after – helping customers create more value.

I feel that if a discussion around technology is needed, it is around the design and implementation of close-the-loop programs. The major reason is that you'll likely be using the same platform when you put it on steroids and transform it into a PPPS program. This will allow you to contact customers proactively and reach all of your customers, instead of only those who complain or reply to surveys.

There are many excellent customer experience measurement and management platforms in the market already, ranging from the very simple and easy-to-implement ones to enterprise-scale platforms that might require six months to make operational. In my experience, the key difference between them lies in their ability to offer good action management.

Whatever solution you choose, you'll probably get a very decent survey builder, i.e., the part of the system that allows you to create and launch your studies. Open- and closed-ended questions — single and multiple answers, grid questions — any platform will offer you the essentials to create a very decent survey. They will also allow you to upload your contacts, send them the survey, and monitor their progress.

In addition, the platforms I've had the opportunity to see also have great reporting capabilities. Dashboards that automatically populate when new data comes in have become the industry standard. If there is a point of differentiation, it is more in the design and user-friendliness than the features they offer. In most platforms, you would get the options to filter results, download them, select time, etc. Anything you need from a good reporting platform will be there.

More substantial differentiation between the CX measurement and management platforms appears when analytics are involved. All will offer the baseline features like distributions and looking at cross-question results. However, there is a difference between the platforms and the more sophisticated features like driver and text analysis. Some truly excel in text analytics and have used it to differentiate from the competitors. Others have embedded many advanced analytical modules that allow you to dig deeper into customers' feedback. Moreover, some have opted to create an app store allowing multiple vendors to connect to their platforms and run analytics or other enhancements on top. Which one you should go for is a matter that's hard to advise on as it is very context-dependent (context here meaning budget and how advanced do you want to go). I'm certain that you won't make a mistake if you go with one of the top 3-4-5 platforms, given that you can afford it.

Finally, the major platforms differ substantially in how action workflows are embedded. What I'd advise you to do when selecting a vendor is to have a very careful look at this part, simply because, as I said, survey builders and reporting capabilities are quite similar, and if need be, you can run analytics outside of the platform. My recommendation is to keep the actions in, and for that, you need to be sure that it can accommodate your requirements. This is more a matter of flexibility than anything else. Close-the-loop programs can differ significantly in the way they are governed and executed. Ideally, a customer experience measurement and management platform would accommodate these differences. For example, some companies might be fine if the person closing the loop takes whatever necessary action to address the customer's feedback. Others might want to make them select from a pre-defined list of actions; still, others might want to get approval from a supervisor before the person closing the loop takes action.

It is such things, in my view, that you'd do well to consider before making a vendor selection.

Integration with external sources is another element that differentiates between the existing platforms, but mostly between the leaders and the others. The leaders would all offer a decent suite of integrations with customer relationship management (CRM) and other systems. Still, check this out as well, as you don't want to be in a situation where you want to input customer data to run an analysis, and you can't do it. Keep in mind, though, that these platforms are not data lakes. They cannot store and offer the same data management as a data lake can, and that's fine if you ask me. Their goal is not to do these things, but to allow you to act, which is yet another reason to focus on what matters – how conducive the technology you are or will be using is.

Ideas for Customer Inspiration, Motivation, Education, and Adjustments on the Fly Initiatives

You've got the commitment, and you've got the technology in place. But how exactly are the people closing the loop going to do it? What do they do when a customer shares negative feedback? There are no bulletproof solutions to this question, but there are some good practices to keep in mind to develop ideas for actions.

If you are just starting your close-the-loop program, it's a good idea to go back to the analytical stage to see which areas have the highest impact on customer satisfaction and which ones most customers are unhappy with. It's a good idea to focus on one of the areas first – it is the low-hanging fruit, and it will make things easier for you.

Once you know which one this is, my advice would be to look for ideas inside your own company. Chances are that this is also an area a lot of people share official complaints about, i.e., your contact center probably receives a lot of those daily. See how they are currently solving these cases. In addition, you might want to run a series of workshops focused on generating ideas for tackling customer dissatisfaction; here, what you learned when you ran analytics on interaction and operational data will prove invaluable. Look at the drivers, look at what people are saying when they share their opinion, and come up with solutions to these as a team. Value-creation is not the responsibility of one team, let alone of one person – it is what customers do with the help of everyone in your company distilled in your product or service. Keep an open mind, as ideas might come from plenty of places and might concern many aspects of your delivery.

Once this is done, you can go live. One thing I don't see enough companies doing is running controlled experiments, similar to A/B testing. If you come up with several possible actions to solve a customer's dissatisfaction, why not test all of them for a certain period and compare the results? For example, maybe many customers complain about long waiting lines for your contact center, and you want to know whether it's better to play music while people are waiting or tell them their queue location. Why not test both? The key here is the accent on 'controlled.' You don't just tell people to do one or the other; put in a little more structure in the process to be sure that you are comparing apples to apples afterward. Oh, and there's no need to test this particular scenario; we already know the answer – queue location works best; call abandonment is almost twice lower, and caller satisfaction is considerably higher with this time filler, compared to music or an apology (Munichor & Rafaeli, 2007).

This latter example reminds me of another way to develop great ideas for your close-the-loop program – know what others are doing. You can do this, for example, by running a mystery shopping study, in which people pretend to be customers of your competitors but are, in reality, gathering competitive intelligence. Before you think about it, there's nothing shady in this practice, as all mystery shoppers can get hold of is already publicly available information, or at the very least, information that the company will be willing to share with actual customers.

I don't know about you, but I've come to realize that a lot of the questions I'm asking myself are already answered by someone. That someone is often a researcher in the academic world. Style of writing aside, monitoring the results of academic studies has many benefits. On the one hand, it's publicly available, unlike most studies paid for by companies. In addition, in most cases, you can be quite certain that the researchers have followed a very rigorous data collection and analysis process. Last but not least, the depth and the specificity of insights are often simply amazing, and academic researchers often investigate questions you wouldn't probably ask yourself. For example, Allen, Brady, Robinson, and Voorhees (Allen et al., 2015) investigated whether a company might benefit from fixing another company's mistakes. Indeed, the "make-up-for-other-companies'-mistakes" effect is real; if an unrelated company has made the customer unhappy, and if you help them, you stand to gain a significant boost in customer satisfaction, repurchase intention, and word-of-mouth.

And finally, stimulating knowledge sharing between teams and sharing success stories can also do miracles in boosting your close-the-loop program's performance. So much knowledge is wasted daily by people not sharing it or leaving the company and taking the knowledge with them; that is painful. Every time this happens, you start from zero. If you can prevent it by building knowledge libraries and sharing success stories, it will benefit both the program and the people involved in its execution. In my professional journey, I've realized that people know a lot, but they share sparingly. Stimulate this sharing process, and you'll quickly discover pockets of gold all over the place.

Return on Investment on Initiatives for Customer Inspiration, Motivation, Education, and Adjustments on the Fly

On to the trickiest of all questions – how do you know that what you are doing is working? Are your close-the-loop actions helping customers create more value? Are they helping your company create more revenue or profit?

These questions are not so difficult to answer analytically; it's more the lack of data points that presents a challenge. There are two ways to estimate the impact of your close-the-loop program. The first one would be to have a look at aggregated data. You put your overall KPI next to business performance indicators and see if they correlate. The problem with this approach is that you probably don't have 30 or preferably sixty-plus quarters of back data for both. And even if you do, it will only tell you that you get more revenue when you increase Net Promoter Score (NPS) or customer satisfaction. You wouldn't know what actions drove that, not to mention that your improved business results might be the outcome of a completely different force at play.

To mitigate these challenges, at least partially, I think it's better to go one level deeper and make the most of the key reason you are running a close-the-loop program using a technology that is up to the task – action tracking. When we spoke earlier about the need for a good action manager, we did that because it is the input that we'll use to figure out what works and what doesn't. The input you need is this: customer feedback at point A, a description of the action that you undertook, and customer feedback at point B. Do this for a long enough time and with a sufficient number of customers, classify the activities into groups to make the analysis doable, and you'll end up with a beautiful dataset of actions and pre- and post-action feedback. Unlike any other analytics, you run a driver analysis (a regression or random forest, or whatever your data scientists deem the best fit), and you will immediately understand which actions work and which don't. You can add account or customer value to the mix for bonus points. Adding the cost of execution will give you a par excellence return on investment calculation.

Does it work in practice? You bet. In 2021, my team won an award for running a similar model for Signify. In 2019, Signify digitized their B2B CX program, driven by the changing B2B environment and customer expectations. All key aspects underwent the digital transformation – feedback collection, insights reporting, and improvement actions. This process unlocked an unprecedented scale and speed of customer insights. Then, the company started seeing the first signs that initial excitement was wearing off. NPS growth was slowing down, and response rates on some markets were decreasing. Signify was challenged to preserve the program's function as a genuine tool for inspiration, internal culture transformation, and continuous improvement. They needed a solution that harnesses the "collective wisdom" already available in the data they gather – the in-depth understanding of the Voice of the Customer within unstructured text feedback and how proactive treatment of the customers' issues through improvement initiatives increases satisfaction.

We developed an algorithm that connects historical data about past improvements with commercial data and gives data-backed suggestions on how an identified issue can be resolved in the most impactful way. Because of the digital transformation they did, Signify has a lot of data available – 105 countries are now actively measuring satisfaction and logging improvements into the platform. Then, we identify which proactive improvements undertaken by Signify executives have had the most significant impact on customers' likelihood to recommend and ultimately – revenue or share of wallet. It is still an ongoing project, but what we discovered is already helping Signify to reach the next stage of its close-the-loop program. For example, we knew that overall NPS for European markets grew by 12 pp in 2020. Still, the impact pilot proved that the positive effect of assigned actions is considerably larger than the NPS increase without clearly defined actions and can be considered a driver of the overall NPS improvement. These findings led to a new, more mature cultural buy-in into the customer-centric philosophy. The latest analytical efforts helped Signify executives move to a holistic customer journey mindset and focus their efforts beyond product quality.

In addition, the numbers also support their conviction to spend time not only on short-term resolutions but also on deeper transformations. Yes, close-the-loop and short-term improvements help the company demonstrate a human face and empathize with customer issues. However, long-term strategic improvements demonstrate that Signify means business, and they are not afraid to turn an entire process on its head because of the customers.

In brief, during the action phase of your PPPS program, it is vital to act on customers' feedback and do it in a way that allows you to monitor the impact of your actions. Four elements contribute considerably to a close-the-loop programs' success: commitment from the management team and the people working in the program; having the right technology in place; having good, diverse ideas about the actions you can take and the appropriate approach to experimenting with them; and running action analytics to understand what works and what doesn't, and to calculate return on investment. You are all set to proceed to the final phase of the PPPS journey.

References

Ajzen, I., & Schmidt, P. (2020). Changing behavior using the theory of planned behavior. In M. Hagger, L. Cameron, K. Hamilton, N. Hankonen, & T. Lintunen (Eds.), *The handbook of behavior change* (Cambridge Handbooks in Psychology, pp. 17–31). Kindle Edition. Cambridge: Cambridge University Press. doi:10.1017/9781108677318.002

Allen, A. M., Brady, M. K., Robinson, S. G., & Voorhees, C. M. (2015). One firm's loss is another's gain: Capitalizing on other firms' service failures. *Journal of the Academy of Marketing Science*, 43(5), 648–662. doi:10.1007/s11747-014-0413-6

McKinsey & Company. (2021a). Prediction: The future of CX. Retrieved from www.mckinsey.com/business-functions/marketing-and-sales/our-insights/prediction-the-future-of-cx

Munichor, N., & Rafaeli, A. (2007, March). Numbers or apologies? Customer reactions to telephone waiting time fillers. *Journal of Applied Psychology*, 92(2), 511–518. doi:10.1037/0021-9010.92.2.511, PMID: 17371095.

Ventura, S. (2021). Survey: The state of journey management and CX measurement. Retrieved from www.pointillist.com/blog/cx-survey-2021-journey-management-cx-measurement/#quantifying-roi-remains-top-cx-challenge

10 Roadmap Step 6 – Scale-Up

Expand Your Initiatives to Your Full Customer Base

What Is the Purpose of This Stage?

We got to the point of doing amazing stuff for your customers in a personalized yet still reactive mode and limited to those who reply to surveys. The last step of the process is to learn from everything we have done so far, gather all the data and insights, and unlock proactive, personalized post-sales service at scale. This is what, without any exaggeration, puts all of your efforts and successes so far on steroids.

I propose that you develop two elements at this final stage. The first one is an algorithm that infers customers' feedback without asking them to share it; the second is a recommendation engine for your actions to go hand in hand with the increased scale. Both of these final but critical touches of your proactive personalized post-sales service (PPPS) program are enabled by predictive analytics.

Scaling Up

Now that you know how to deal with unhappy customers, it's time to expand. Seeing the return on investment of their close-the-loop program, many companies do the most natural thing and look for ways to do more of it. The challenge they face is the two icebergs – the customer complaint and the survey response ones. With the best of intentions and the most effective efforts, you will not be able to reach 100% of your customers; if we are honest, you probably won't reach even 50%, and in most cases, even much less. This leaves you with a fundamentally limited perspective of your customer base. You just don't know what most of your customers think of you and your products or services. There is a way of filling in this huge gap, and it is by inferring customer feedback based on what they do or go through.

At this point, you have in your hands a data lake that consists of customer feedback, usage, interaction, operational, external, and customer background data. We already used this data set to understand what makes people evaluate your products and services in one way or another, i.e., to reveal the drivers of customer evaluation.

DOI: 10.4324/9781003309284-13

Figure 10.1 From a limited to a full-customer-base view of customer evaluation.

The process of inferring how customers who hadn't complained or replied to surveys evaluate your products or services is very similar to running this driver analysis. In essence, we are looking for markers of satisfaction or dissatisfaction among customers whose evaluation we know, and using them to infer how those whose evaluation we don't know are likely to feel.

The difference between the two is not so much in the actual analysis, but rather in its interpretation and application. When we looked at the drivers of satisfaction or dissatisfaction, we interpreted the results as "This is causing customers to think that", for example, "The experience with the FAQ section on our website is making customers dissatisfied". We could then consider whether improving the FAQ section should be a priority or not. When we look to infer customer satisfaction or dissatisfaction, we use these insights to apply them to customers whose evaluation we don't know.

In practical terms, your customer data set is (most likely) considerably bigger than your customer evaluation one. This is because if you have the right technology in place, you are likely to have operational, interaction, and all other types of customer data for all of your customers, yet because of the survey response iceberg you don't know how all customers feel about your products and services. It is this smaller set of customers for which you have both their evaluation and customer data that is the foundation of the predictive analytics you'll be running, as these are the customers for which you know everything.

Out of this set of customers for which you know both their feedback and their customer data, you or the people who would be running the analysis will have to take about 20% into a separate set of data – this is your validation set, i.e., the results against which you'll be judging the effectiveness of your predictive algorithm. The remainder 80% of the data set will be your training set.

What happens next is the development of a model that links customer data with customer feedback. It is beyond the scope of the book to go into

Step 1. Build a customer data lake

CUSTOMER EVALUATION

CUSTOMER DATA

Step 2. Identify customer data that can be used to infer customer evaluation

Step 3. Infer customer evaluation from customer data

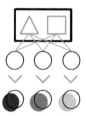

Figure 10.2 Inferring customer evaluation based on customer data.

the technical details; me and my team have done this by using a gradient-boosting technique, but this is just one of doing this – there is a plethora of machine-learning techniques that can do the job.

At the next step, this model is essentially turned on its head – instead of looking at which customer data points drive customer evaluation, we do it the other way around and infer the evaluation based on the customer data. This is done on the validation data set we left aside previously – we run the predictive algorithm on this latter set and measure its accuracy against the ground truth, i.e., what we actually know about customers.

I feel that a word of caution is needed here. This whole process is by no means perfect or 100% accurate. In my experience, 80% accuracy is achievable with a good data set, but even if it's lower (50% or 60%), there is a good business sense of doing this exercise, as it still points you in the right direction.

Once you have done this, what you have in your hands is your full customer base with a tag next to each customer indicating whether they are satisfied or dissatisfied (or a promoter or a detractor, depending on the customer feedback indicator you are using). What this unlocks is the way of working with customers that we've been advocating for throughout the whole book – being proactive and addressing customer needs in a personalized fashion. Your company can now start contacting customers you know are unhappy to try and alleviate the dissatisfaction; by the same token, you can also start contacting happy customers to boost word-of-mouth and gain more recommendations. The benefits you gain from this can, without exaggeration, be huge, as the success stories we'll see later in this chapter show.

Action Recommendation Engine

Before we move to showcasing the impact of doing PPPS at scale, it would be beneficial to spend a few minutes talking about a second predictive algorithm that might come in very handy at this stage – an action recommendation engine. While it is not a must at this stage, I would strongly recommend that you develop one. At the smaller scale at which your close-the-loop program is before you predict customer feedback, your mistakes are also smaller. When you scale it up, though, everything matters much more. For example, if you are not taking the most effective and efficient steps to tackle customer dissatisfaction, the impact is now multiplied by the bigger scale of your program.

To manage this better, I consider it a good idea to develop an action recommendation engine for the people who are closing the loop to use as a guide. At the end of the previous stage of the process, we examined the impact of your actions on customer experience or customer satisfaction. You can take this one step further and turn this knowledge into an active guidance system for your colleagues.

The logic of building it is fundamentally the same as the one that goes into the recommendation systems of the Netflixes and Amazons of this world – you look at what worked with other customers with the same profile and recommend actions based on this. A simple example: imagine that you know that when 30-40-year-old customers living in London are unhappy with your service, it's mostly because of the pricing. You have tested several solutions to this – an outright discount, or keeping the same price but putting them in a higher service tier, or sending them a Thank you gift – and you've discovered that sending them a gift works best. An action recommendation engine reads all the background information from your data lake and recommends a list of actions to the person who is proactively addressing customer needs. In addition, you can also match contact center representatives with customers and their specific feedback so that people who are good at solving customer issues related to pricing deal with these issues. Further, those who handle conversations better should be assigned to handle these conversations.

All in all, an action recommendation engine is helpful for scaling up your proactive personalized post-sales service program. It gives the people interacting with customers a good guidance on the actions that are likely to make an impact, thus increasing the return on investment on your program.

Success Stories

The things we discussed so far might seem farfetched to you. At first glance, saying that we can predict the future could sound preposterous – that's an almost God-like power. Yet, it is not something that hadn't been done before or something you haven't encountered in practice already. At the beginning of the second section of this book, we reviewed several academic research publications that inferred or predicted music success, photo preferences, and even personality traits without asking people for them. And if you've seen Amazon's or Netflix's recommendation engines, you have encountered something very similar as well. With the limitations posed by people's free will, predicting or inferring their behavior and attitudes is quite possible.

I want to offer you an alternative ending to this chapter because we already saw many mechanics of inferring customer feedback and building an action recommendation engine in practice. Instead of a 'How to' section that suggests the nitty-gritty things to consider, I'd like to offer you two success stories that will give you a glimpse of what predicting customer feedback can do for you.

The first example comes from BAIN, the company that created and owns the Net Promoter Score (NPS) trademark. In their words,

> We worked with a financial services firm to build a model that predicts the likely outcome of a telephone call placed to the customer service center. We gathered operational metrics surrounding the call (such as hold time, talk time, and number of transfers), the customer's recent transactions, and her digital footprint. In addition, we deployed advanced natural language processing algorithms to analyze the call transcript to extract call reason, intent, and sentiment. Finally, we fed these sets of structured and unstructured data into a number of machine learning algorithms, using labeled NPS data as the target variable.
>
> The results: an overall accuracy above 80% for predicting NPS status, and a fourfold lift above the baseline in identifying detractors. We also identified key drivers for each individual prediction via techniques such as Local Interpretable Model-Agnostic Explanations (LIME) and SHapley Additive exPlanations (SHAP). These local model interpretability methods informed more tailored actions at the individual customer level, including targeted callbacks by frontline managers.
>
> (Carikcioglu, 2021)

In my practice, the team I have had the opportunity to work with has done this at a bigger scale for several telecommunication companies. UPC Switzerland already had a very impactful close-the-loop program when we started working with them. Using one of the leading CX measurement and management platforms, they collected a large amount of customer feedback per month across many domains – from relationships (i.e., the overall company level), through product, to touchpoints/interactions. This information was constantly fed to their contact center teams, which addressed the feedback from extremely unhappy customers. The results were in place, and they were successfully retaining a portion of these customers who would have otherwise left the company.

The big challenge for UPC was that the program lacked the scale. With the success of the close-the-loop program naturally came the appetite to do more, but there was no way to scale it up, simply because they weren't receiving more feedback from customers. Then, a thought occurred to one of our contacts at UPC – what if we don't need customers to tell us how they feel? What if we can infer it from what we already know? This sparked what later would become a solution that has received industry-wide recognition by winning several CX and data science awards.

To achieve that, we had a very good reading on the customers' data that UPC lawfully collects. Luckily, they are very advanced in data management and have managed to break down organizational silos that very often limit data availability, so that wasn't difficult to get. We ended up with a huge data set of 1,200 variables of historical usage and interaction data, ranging from mobile internet usage to whether customers pay their bills on time. We added customers' feedback to this pool of information to use it as a target variable, i.e., what we wanted to infer.

Next, we split the data set in two. Ten percent of it we left aside; this served as the 'ground truth' – the actual numbers that we'll compare our predictions to later on. On the other 90% of the data, we applied a machine-learning model using a gradient-boosting technique chosen because of its robustness to avoid over-fitting of predictions and, at the same time, consider the multiple interactions in the process and easily handle missing data. It was generally preferred because of its overall accuracy compared to other loss functions considered.

This model linked customer feedback (in this case – NPS) to all other data UPC has for its customers and allowed us to see which variables are most informative about negative or positive customer feedback. Once developed, we tested it against the ground truth to realize, with gusto, that it achieves 80% accuracy in predicting super-detractors, as UPC calls them – people replying with 0 or 1 on the willingness to recommend survey scale used to measure NPS. An accuracy level of 80% might not sound like much, but in practice, it means a seven times higher likelihood of identifying a super-detractor compared to chance.

At the final step of the process, we applied, and still do, this model on the vast pool of customers over which UPC has no visibility because they haven't shared their feedback. With this, UPC proactively contacted customers for whom we know there's a good chance of being super-detractors to try and alleviate dissatisfaction. In the pilot stage, they decreased churn by 34% in the treated population vs. non-treated control groups. In the first year, by saving customers who would have otherwise left, UPC was able to secure five times more revenue than the program's cost. Since then, this approach was expanded to include other countries in which Liberty Global (the owner of UPC Switzerland) operates, such as Germany and the UK.

If you imagine a way of expanding the scope of your knowledge three-fold or fivefold overnight, this is exactly what this last step of the PPPS program does for you. It puts your efforts to contribute to your customers' value-creation process on a foundation of completely different sizes. This quantum leap is made possible by the boom in data availability, by applying world-class analytics, and by having the willingness and ability to do what's right. Before we close this book, I'd like to briefly mention some challenges you might face while traveling on the PPPS journey and share best practices for tackling them.

Reference

Carikcioglu, I. (2021). Sidestepping survey fatigue, predictive NPS gets to the heart of customers' attitudes. Retrieved from www.bain.com/insights/sidestepping-survey-fatigue-predictive-nps-gets-to-the-heart-of-customers-attitudes/

11 Challenges in Designing and Running Proactive Personalized Post-Sales Service Programs

Undoubtedly, there are many challenges companies will face when offering proactive, personalized post-sales service (PPPS). Some of them, the ones related to taking the steps that take you there, we discussed in the last few chapters.

Getting buy-in from the people the execution of a PPPS program depends on is always somewhat of a challenge, simply because doing change management is always difficult. You can vastly improve your chances of success on this point if you: bring the outside in, act with urgency, build a guiding coalition, look for opportunities in crisis, and find a way to deal with NoNos.

A similar organizational challenge is posed by the desire (and requirement) to collect customer data, connect all its pieces on the one hand, and customer feedback data on the other. Organizational siloes and often the simple unwillingness of people to support this process might occur as obstacles. The data, in my experience, is almost always there. The challenge is getting to it.

Ensuring the validity and reliability of all data points you will be using to predict customer behavior is a challenge of a different nature. While the previous two were related to dealing with other people, this one is more analytical and concerns your and your vendors' ability to make the right decisions regarding customer feedback and customer data collection, and running the right analytics.

Even when you are past this point, you could still face challenges related to the inner workings of your organization when you reach the stage of implementing the findings from your analyses; that is, when you start acting to contribute to the customer value-creation process. From training people to resistance from other managers, a lot can happen at this stage to sabotage your efforts.

Finally, understanding which of the actions you've taken actually work and creating a system to allow you to expand them to your full customer base is no walk in the park either. In fact, measuring the return on investment (ROI) of our actions has for decades been the ultimate challenge for CX marketing practitioners alike. And even when you know what works and what doesn't, expanding it to your full customer base, i.e., predicting customer behavior, could be challenging from a purely analytical perspective.

DOI: 10.4324/9781003309284-14

After all, as the saying goes, "it is difficult to make predictions, especially about the future".

These are all challenges a company is likely to face on the road to PPPS from an internal perspective; they all concern either the inner workings of your organization or the intricacies of data management and analytics. Before concluding this book, we should say a few words about the PPPS-related challenges you might face when dealing with customers.

In one of the seminal articles on proactive post-sales service, Challagalla et al. (2009) summarized the findings from nine focus groups with a total of 84 managers (B2B and B2C). This study was conducted to understand the dimensions of proactive post-sales service, the expected outcomes, and the challenges managers faced or expected to face. These include:

- Motive uncertainty: unclarity on customer's end whether the company is reaching out with altruistic (to help) or egoistic (to sell) intentions.
- Privacy: the amount and type of data companies collect about their customers is only one part of this. Perhaps the bigger issue will be how companies can avoid the impression that they are intruding in people's lives.
- Lack of empathy: A significant challenge when implementing large-scale programs at companies is ensuring that service reps act with authenticity and empathy. Who among us hadn't been in a call initiated by a company in which the contact person is clearly following a script almost without paying attention to our answers?
- Time and frequency of contact: In a world in which we all receive dozens of notifications and tons of information that requires our attention, how often and when exactly companies reach out to customers becomes a vital question to be answered.
- Last, providing excellent service will raise the bar as customers' expectations will increase. This is not necessarily a bad thing, as the new, higher expectations will also be in place for your competitors. Still, it is something for companies to consider.
- B2B specific: the lack of a single decision-maker poses the question "Whom should companies work with on the customer's side? Whom should they proactively engage with?"

If I told you that there are silver bullets for these challenges, I'd be lying or at least assuming an arrogant position. But this also doesn't mean that there are no ways to mitigate the impact of these challenges. We will have a look at them one by one below. But first, the ultimate solution.

Drumroll for the most effective, widely appreciated, and bulletproof way of tackling all the challenges listed above – contribute to customers' lives by helping them create more value with what they've purchased from you. If there is a solution that makes all the challenges void, it is this.

- If you do that, customers will have no reason to doubt your intentions, or at the very least, would be appreciative.

- If you do that, customers will have fewer concerns about data privacy because they are getting something out of it (known in the academic literature as the 'privacy calculus').
- If you do that, your employees will feel better because you'll be giving them a purpose.
- If you do that, time and frequency of contact concerns will lessen in strength or vanish. After all, you are helping people; you might be doing it a tad too often, but I'm certain that people will understand or will at least share their feedback with you.
- If you do that, customer expectations will indeed increase. And that works in your favor! Everyone else will be judged against the criteria set by you.
- If you do that, it doesn't matter too much if you cover all the important stakeholders within a company. They talk to each other. They'll do the work for you if you help them do your work.

Beyond this, you can do several other things to tackle the implementation challenges in front of PPPS. We discuss them in turn in the following pages.

Motive Uncertainty

It is only natural for customers to harbor suspicion as to why the company is reaching out to them, be it to collect feedback, prevent an issue, or educate them. With so many sales calls and emails going around, who would not doubt the reason for yet another call or email offering to help while trying to sell something? At the heart of the issue lies a lack of trust between the company and the customer. How do you solve this? One thing I've seen working well in practice is being upfront with the customer. I'm not saying that they'll believe you, at least not the first time, maybe. Still, it does put the conversation on a different level, and with enough skill on the customer service rep, it might make the interaction open and honest.

Second, nothing solves trust issues better than consistent experience pointing in the right direction. The first time you reach out to a customer, they might be suspicious. But if they see that you do as you say and are not trying to sell them anything, and if this repeats a couple of more times, trust will naturally start emerging. Consistency is vital in the process, and it has the added benefit of making customers less annoyed when they receive a call or an email from you. With the repetition, customers will likely get used to having this interaction with you, will open up, and might even look forward to it. Now that's a place you want to be.

Privacy

This is perhaps the biggest obstacle companies that adopt the PPPS framework will face. As privacy concerns continue to escalate, customers will become much more knowledgeable and careful in sharing their data with companies. One thing that might mitigate customers' concerns is implementing an opt-in process for at least part of the data. A good example in this direction comes from Microsoft, asking you what kind of data you would like to share with them.

Most companies are lagging in explaining why they are gathering this data. And I have to say, "to show you more relevant ads" doesn't make for a compelling case, at least for yours truly. Now, I don't mind this 'benefit' if it comes along with 'we will send you personalized advice to help you advance your photographic skills'. Even better, I'd love to see example content and how you plan to deliver it to me. Oh, and a note on how you ensure security would also be a nice touch. I'm giving these examples merely to make the point that a bit more explanation, combined with the old-fashioned being relevant and helpful, can do miracles in convincing customers why it is a good idea to share their data with you. The answer is, in essence, so that you can help the customer back, not only for your benefit.

We need to look no further for evidence that privacy concerns can be alleviated by helping people create value than Chris Meadows's story we saw earlier. Here's what he, as a customer, says about it:

> Some people might find this disturbing from a privacy standpoint, but on the other hand, it stands to reason that any system where things could go wrong would have some kind of self-monitoring setup built-in, just so it could tell if people were having trouble somewhere and a server needed to be rebooted or something.
>
> (Meadows, 2018)

Chris definitely had thoughts about his privacy being violated – after all, if it was a non-issue, he wouldn't be writing about it. Yet, he is understanding. He looks at the company's perspective and deems its action reasonable. I can't help but think that this is so because Amazon is proactively adjusting things on the fly, thus helping him create value – watch a movie with a friend.

Lack of Empathy

Surface acting on the side of contact representatives is always a challenge on the side of companies. The best practices that are generally available for mitigating this remain applicable in PPPS. One option is to "Institute policies and 'display rules' that encourage the delivery of emphatic service" (Challagalla et al., 2009, 82). While I'm not against this solution, it merely makes people better actors but doesn't mean they won't act. We all know that it shows when you are just the next person the service rep needs to call; even with the best intentions, you can feel it in their tone of voice and formal behavior. Perhaps the next level of solving this is to embed your team members' jobs with purpose and meaning that goes beyond achieving key performance indicators (KPIs) and meeting targets. If your goal is to support the customer in creating more value, and if your content and actions work in this direction, then it becomes much easier for service reps to convey this message. They can be their authentic selves because they are there to help the customer and not merely to tick a box in a customer relationship management (CRM).

Time and Frequency of Contact

This is perhaps the easiest of all implementation challenges to tackle. The potential damage if you don't get this right is high, there's no doubt about it. Customers may get annoyed and start avoiding any interaction with you altogether; not an enviable position to be in. On the positive side, though, you can adopt at least two solutions.

On the one hand, if there is one area where you can start small and grow from there, it is this. After all, no requirement says you need to launch your PPPS program for all customers at once; and what's even better, you can start with a lower frequency of contact, gauge the interest, and intensify it if there is such. Clearly, you can also, and that's the way I'd recommend, run a limited field experiment – set aside a group of customers and start with a low contact frequency. For maximum impact, you can also tell them that you are testing this mode of engagement – unless you only have unhappy customers, which means you are probably no longer in business, you will be able to find a group of customers willing to cooperate. And then test and ask for feedback until you get this right.

In addition, data analytics can come to the rescue on this point. Remember when we spoke earlier about understanding which of your actions work and which don't, and how you can analyze and measure their ROI? Well, part of this exercise, in my view, should always be the tweaking of mechanics of actions so that they can deliver higher impact; time and frequency of contact are nothing but action mechanics. If you have collected action data properly and included it in your analysis of actions that contribute to a better customer experience, knowing how often and when to contact your customers should be apparent to you.

Customers' Expectations Will Increase

I've heard this one before in different contexts, and it always made me wonder. Will you shy away from doing something good for your customers and your business because they'll get used to it and will want more? I understand the logic behind it, and there's certainly some merit to this thinking. Yet, I'm not sure it leads to positive results. After all, if you don't do it, someone else will. And instead of you setting the bar, you will be playing catch with your competitors. It's more a matter of who drives customer expectations up, rather than if they will go up. I'm merely claiming that it's better if you do it.

The Lack of a Single Decision-Maker (in B2B Contexts)

This is a challenge inherent in making B2B sales, and one that is solvable following the best practices in key account management. Stakeholder mapping is, from my perspective, a must, as well as mapping the stakeholder relationships, especially related to the process of buying and using the product. You will have to help most, if not all of them, accomplish their respective goals. Clearly, the task is made more difficult because of the engagement scale. At the same time, unlike, for example, physical product-based B2C businesses that have limited interactions with customers and it's more difficult to collect deep data, in B2B environments, the company–customer relationship is often closer and warmer making it easier to understand customer needs in detail.

I appreciate that none of these challenges related to your interaction with customers during PPPS are easy to solve. The roadmap of PPPS also poses some tricky questions, such as getting buy-in, collecting and collating all the customer data, measuring ROI of your actions, and predicting customer behavior. Yet, none of these are insurmountable difficulties. Some companies are on their way; others have already arrived and see the benefits of offering PPPS to customers. With the right approach and the will to overcome challenges to future-proof your business, you can also get there. The future is here.

References

Challagalla, G., Venkatesh, R., & Kohli, A. K. (2009). Proactive postsales service: When and why does it pay off? *Journal of Marketing*, 73(2), 70–87. doi:10.1509/jmkg.73.2.70

Meadows, C. (2018). An unexpected Amazon refund demonstrates just how clever Jeff Bezos can be. Retrieved from https://teleread.org/2018/05/06/an-unexpected-amazon-refund-demonstrates-just-how-clever-jeff-bezos-can-be/

Recap

When the idea of inferring customer feedback without using surveys and basing it only on usage and interaction data came up in conversations with Liberty Global a couple of years ago, I thought that was crazy. By education, I'm a sociologist. I'm not oblivious to the desire to know what will happen next. I'm certainly a supporter of the idea that science, and any other research for that matter, serves a single purpose – to predict the future. Yet, somehow the idea of quantifying these predictions, giving them a specific numerical expression, left if not a preposterous, then at least an uncomfortable ring in my ear.

How, I wondered, would we do that? Do they imagine the amount of data we would need? And I wasn't even sure we'd get anything that makes sense. We do research, i.e., we explore unchartered territories, and sometimes, the insight that we get is that there is no path through this territory. When a client expects you to tell them what's driving customer satisfaction, you can't tell them that none of the data you or they have is in any way predictive of it, can you? With experience, you learn to handle this. But this request was so new that neither the team nor I knew what we would do if nothing came out of the algorithm.

As it happened, the project was a huge success; the market moved in the same direction a couple of years after we completed the project, and we struck gold.

The more the team and I dug, the more interesting things started to appear – the project we did was just one piece of a much larger field that an increasing number of companies are entering right now. It took years to understand all of the repercussions of what it means that we could infer customer feedback without surveys. How do we scale this up? How does this fit with other things our clients are doing? What else can we do to support them? These are all questions my colleagues and I struggled to answer.

At a certain point in this process, the fog started to withdraw, pushed aside by a conceptual lens that put things into focus. We came to realize what that bigger picture was about. In marketing lingo, it is, "Every company should be able to proactively address customer needs". In more academic terms, I call it proactive personalized post-sales service (PPPS).

PPPS is an inherently customer-centric perspective developed after the Service-Dominant Logic paradigm in marketing. Central to both is the acknowledgment that, from a company perspective, a post-sales process is for the customer when they create value with the products or services they bought. Because of this, if they want to create value with their propositions, companies can only do it through their customers and not on their own; from this perspective, what we often like to say, that we deliver value, is plain wrong. We can only deliver the tools for someone else to create value; the customer is always a co-creator.

Following this thread, there are three groups of things companies can do to support customers in their value-creation process: they can improve their products and services at large; they can boost the value-creation process by inspiring, motivating, and educating customers on how to put the products and services to better use; and they can remove barriers to value-creation by making adjustments to their products or service on the fly, for example, when they repair or replace a product. Here, we focused on the latter two types of actions, as there's already a plethora of writings on how to (further) develop products and services.

Garmin provides a great example of doing proactive education at scale. Their smart watches gather heart rate data all the time, in every single second. Analyzing this data, they came up with metrics derived from this single indicator, and they offer them to most of their customers (depending on the class of watch they buy). The beauty of this is that you get (fairly) personalized insights. For example, you wouldn't get advice about the importance of sleeping well; you would get it when you haven't slept well. Similarly, they will advise you to get some rest because a stressful day delayed your recovery only when this happens, and not simply in a newsletter you receive once a week. Garmin doesn't have to educate you to use their watch. They help you be a better version of yourself.

For example, Amazon is known for proactively addressing potential customer dissatisfaction. We saw what kind of impression this left on a customer who got refunded 3$. The attitude got appreciated the most and the desire to be there when a customer needs you, not the refund itself. It simply creates trust. If a company is willing to give you back some money because they've done something wrong, it is certainly worthy of our appreciation, isn't it?

These two, boosting value-creation and removing barriers, work best when done proactively, personalized, and scalable. Many studies, academic and otherwise, and thought-leaders prove these points.

Retana et al. (2015) showed that proactively educating customers leads to 3% points lower churn and 20% fewer questions. Shin et al. (2017) measured customer satisfaction in a proactive vs. reactive mode of providing support and discovered that it's considerably higher when the company preemptively addressed potential issues. Additionally, Voorhees et al. (2006) found that repurchase intention among people who were dissatisfied with their service was the highest among those who received a company-initiated recovery.

Ball et al. (2006) discovered that personalization leads to higher satisfaction and trust, which leads to loyalty, and other studies corroborate their findings. These results are also echoed by business consultants like McKinsey, who report that 71% of consumers expect personalization, and 76% get frustrated when a company "…shows or recommends [them] things that are not relevant…" (McKinsey & Company, 2021).

And finally, you can expect the highest business result and help customers the most when you can do proactive and personalized post-sales service at scale, i.e., to deliver it to all customers.

The way companies are currently doing post-sales service does not cut to the chase. Existing solutions are either reactive, or not personalized, or offer limited scale, or a combination of these.

When you rely on complaint management to offer adjustments on the fly, you are reacting to customers' feedback and will also encounter the customer complaint iceberg – a very limited number of your unhappy customers will contact you.

When you do a close-the-loop program in which you initiate the contact, get feedback, and act on it, you are actively collecting information. However, you are still a step behind as you rely on customers sharing feedback, and you encounter the survey response iceberg – not every customer will reply to a survey.

Finally, you can also boost value-creation by offering inspiration, motivation, and education at scale via product manuals and tutorials, frequently asked questions sections on websites, and so on. While these pass the scale test, they are also reactive and generic ways to do PPPS.

Despite these challenges, the leaders in PPPS still manage to design and develop successful programs. How do they do it? The short answer is that they make the most of opportunities to create more and better data, manage it appropriately, and apply state-of-the-art analytics. This allows them to answer the paramount question to PPPS – how can we predict or infer customers' feedback without asking them.

The roadmap I suggest that you follow consists of a handful of more or less easy-to-follow steps. I suggest you start by laying out a good plan for getting from ground zero to a full-scale PPPS program and set goals, milestones, and priorities. This will make it much easier for you to understand where you stand at every step of the way. Getting buy-in from budget holders, if you are not one, will also be critical at the first step. You can, of course, skip these steps and do it on a piece-by-piece basis, yet I believe that there is a lot of value in having and being able to show a fully developed, longer-term vision.

Once these are in place, it's time to lay the foundations of PPPS by getting data in. There are two ingredients that you need. The first one is customer feedback – how do customers think and feel when using your products and services? The second one is customer data you can gather by either tracking customer behavior or asking them. Customer data has five elements, and while it's not necessary to have tons of each, my advice would be to try and get as much as possible in; these are usage, interaction, operational, external, and customer background data.

Data validity and reliability are key requirements at this initial stage of PPPS. Still, the one thing that can block your progress even if you meet them is the ability to link the different pieces of data together. At a later stage, we'd infer customer feedback from the data you own about customers alone. Therefore, you must ensure all the pieces of data can be connected.

With this data set that you've built, you can start understanding the reasons behind customer feedback. You can add to a plethora of analyses to come up with the drivers of customer satisfaction, and these will be invaluable at the next stage when you act to increase it.

Once you have a good idea of what customers think and the areas for improvement, you can start making steps to boost the value-creation process and remove barriers in front of it. In a word, this is the time to develop a close-the-loop program, in which you act on a one-to-one basis to influence customer feedback in a positive direction. Make sure that you have an organizational commitment and you are always on the lookout for ideas that will make your customers happier and get the right technology in place. Action management is vital here, and I'd recommend that you have a good way of tracking what actions are taken, by whom, and so on. This will allow you, in time, to get a good view of which actions work and which don't.

All of what we did so far prepared us to move to the final step in developing your PPPS program – becoming proactive and scaling it up. After the previous stage, you are still acting reactively, and you are still not covering all your customers. This is so because, as we saw, close-the-loop programs are dependent on customer feedback, and not every one of your customers will share it with you. At this final step of the process, you put together customer feedback and the rest of the customer data to build an algorithm that automatically detects that a customer might be unhappy. This algorithm is then applied to the data you already own, i.e., all of the customer data we gathered earlier and indicated the attitude of every customer. Ideally, you would supplement this with an action recommendation engine, developed on top of your actions and kept good track of at the previous stage. With this, you can now start proactively addressing their needs and scaling up your program enormously, with spectacular results for your business and your customers.

Some companies are already there. We saw that the likes of Amazon, Garmin, and Adobe have similar programs in place, and we reviewed in more detail the program Liberty Global built by inferring customer feedback and acting on it at scale. You will be facing certain challenges at every step of the process, yet these are not unsurmountable. I hope this book offers a good starting point for asking more questions and looking for ways to address customers' needs proactively.

For me, books are perspectives. This one is no different – it merely offers one way of looking at things. I hope I'm correct in pinpointing PPPS as an opportunity for companies to create a win–win situation with their customers. It is always good to be right. Hearing someone say that you are correct in saying something or that they agree with you has such a nice ring. Who among us doesn't cherish the energy and ego boost that comes with it? I, for one, do – I love to be right!

Yet, like it or not, I'm often wrong. I make mistakes, miss important points of view, don't give good enough examples, and whatnot. I hope you will forgive me when you encounter such in this book.

Books are perspectives, and perspectives are muscles – we use them, or we lose them. My sincere hope is that this book will not leave you indifferent. I hope I've managed to develop it, spark your imagination, and contribute to your thinking. If there is a question on your mind, related to PPPS or not, when you close the book that wasn't there before, then this book has achieved its purpose.

And finally, in the true spirit of PPPS, I'd love to hear from you; do reach out to share feedback, exchange ideas, or simply grab a coffee. Interesting perspectives to business, and life more broadly, are always just around the corner.

References

Ball, D., Coelho, P. S., & Vilares, M. J. (2006). Service personalization and loyalty. *Journal of Services Marketing*, 20(6), 391–403. doi:10.1108/08876040610691284

McKinsey & Company. (2021). The value of getting personalization right—Or wrong—Is multiplying. Retrieved from www.mckinsey.com/business-functions/marketing-and-sales/our-insights/the-value-of-getting-personalization-right-or-wrong-is-multiplying

Retana, G. F., Forman, C., & Wu, D. J. (2015, April 26). Proactive customer education, customer retention, and demand for technology support: Evidence from a field experiment. *Manufacturing and Service Operations Management*. Available at SSRN. Retrieved from https://ssrn.com/abstract=2430012 or http://dx.doi.org/10.2139/ssrn.2430012

Shin, H., Ellinger, A. E., Mothersbaugh, D. L., & Reynolds, K. E. (2017). Employing proactive interaction for service failure prevention to improve customer service experiences. *Journal of Service Theory and Practice*, 27(1), 164–186. https://doi.org/10.1108/JSTP-07-2015-0161

Voorhees, C. M., Brady, M. K., & Horowitz, D. M. (2006, October). A voice from the silent masses: An exploratory and comparative analysis of noncomplainers. *Journal of the Academy of Marketing Science*, 34(4), 514–527. doi:10.1177/0092070306288762

Supplemental Material

Q&A

In this section, I'll offer brief answers to proactive personalized post-sales (PPPS)-related questions I've been asked by clients in conversations. Most of these we already touched upon in previous chapters – the purpose of this section is to serve as something you can quickly and easily refer to without skimming through the full length of the book.

Should I Worry This Much About Post-Sales Service?

I think so. Post-sales service is only from your perspective; it is an inherently company-centric term. From a customer perspective, this is when they actually work with your proposition to create value for themselves.

Why Proactive Post-Sales Service?

Because the impact of post-sales service is considerably higher when you initiate it, compared to when a customer does.

Why Personalized Post-Sales Service?

Similar to the benefits of being proactive, personalized post-sales service works better because you are being much more relevant to your customers. Generic solutions are a thing of the past. The future is personalized.

Do I Need All of This Data? I Worry That It Might Take Me Too Much Effort to Get It

No, you don't necessarily need all of the data we spoke about. However, you must have customer feedback and customer data, be it usage, interaction, operational, external, or background. Inferring customer feedback can be done by any of these alone (except external data), but it works better if you can have at least some bits and pieces from all areas. There is a good likelihood that this data already exists somewhere in the organization. I've often seen finding and getting access to it as more of a challenge than creating it. You can start small and work your way from there.

Does This Mean That Complaint Management and Close-the-Loop Initiatives I Have in Place Are Worthless?

Not at all! PPPS is an upgrade to them, not a replacement. By inferring customers' feedback, you can become proactive, instead of reactive, you can target your actions much better to fit individual customers' needs, and you can do it at scale.

What If We Don't Have a Good Close-the-Loop Program in Place? What If We Can't Act Quickly Enough on Customer Feedback?

My advice would be to get this done before moving on to a scaled-up program. If you can't act on what customers are sharing with you, knowing the opinion of all of your customers is just good-to-know information.

How Accurately Can We Infer Customer Feedback?

Eighty percent would be doable given a good enough data set to use as a starting point. I'd be happy with 60–65% as well, and I believe there is a limited benefit for investing in pushing it over 85%.

Doesn't This Whole Business with Inferring Feedback and Collecting Data Drain the Soul Out of It?

I don't think so. If anything, it allows you to have a much bigger impact on customers' lives. It's up to you to make it a positive one.

Is It Legal to Use All This Data?

It is, as long as you have the necessary consent from customers, and you follow General Data Protection Regulation (GDPR). To turn this the other way around, PPPS does not require anything beyond what GDPR permits.

PPPS Ingredients Checklist

The PPPS ingredients checklist gives you an overview of all of the elements you need to have in place to offer proactive personalized post-sales service successfully. It summarizes the requirements we discussed in more detail earlier and is designed to make it easier for you to kick-start a PPPS transformation.

Table S.1 PPPS Ingredients Checklist

Item	Status
Is there buy-in on the vision from budget holders?	
Have you filled in this checklist to understand what you have in place?	
Do you have a plan for gathering the missing pieces?	
Is customer feedback data available?	
Is customer feedback data reliable?	
Is customer feedback data valid?	
Do you collect customers':	

- usage data and/or
- interaction data and/or
- operational data and/or
- external data and/or
- background data.

Is it possible to connect customer feedback with customer data?	
Do you have a good understanding of what's behind customers' feedback, i.e., what's driving their opinions?	
Do you have the commitment to act on customer feedback?	
Do you have the technology to streamline your actions on customer feedback?	
Do you have the technology to monitor your actions on customer feedback?	
Do you have a good understanding of which actions work for maximizing the value customers can create with your proposition?	
Do you have a model that allows you to infer customer feedback without reaching out to customers?	

PPPS Compared to Other Modes of Delivering Post-Sales Service

Table S.2 PPPS Compared to Other Modes of Delivering Post-Sales Service

	Adjustments on the fly: complaint management	Adjustments on the fly: close-the-loop	Customer inspiration, motivation, and education at scale	Proactive personalized post-sales service
Description	A customer complaints to the company about an issue, and the company reacts	The company initiates customer feedback collection and then acts to address it	The company offers inspirational, motivational, and educational materials to all of its customers	Proactively reaching out to customers to address their specific needs and allow them to create more value with the company's proposition. All of this – at scale.
Scale	Only customers who complain – less than 10% of the unhappy ones	Only customers who reply to surveys – typically less than 20%	Potentially all customers	Potentially all customers
Feedback initiated by	Customer	Company	Company	None – identification of customers who need attention is done via predictive analytics based on behavioral, transaction, and other types of data it owns for its customers.
Reactive or proactive	Reactive, after recognition of an issue/recognition of the need	Reactive, after recognition of an issue/recognition of the need	Proactive, before recognition of an issue/recognition of the need	Proactive, before recognition of an issue/recognition of the need
Actions tailored to specific customer's needs	Yes	Yes	No	Yes

(continued)

Table S.2 Cont.

	Adjustments on the fly: complaint management	Adjustments on the fly: close-the-loop	Customer inspiration, motivation, and education at scale	Proactive personalized post-sales service
Adjustments on the fly process	A customer files a complaint about a service failure. The company addresses the issue and takes actions to mitigate the damage.	The company invites customers to participate in a survey. Those who reply can share positive and negative feedback, and the company can then close the loop and follow up on the feedback.	Typically, mass communication about anticipated service failures, such as electricity or broadband interruptions.	The company predicts whether a specific customer is having a negative experience and proactively addresses the issue.
Customer inspiration, motivation, and education process	A customer has a question about using a product to achieve a goal. They contact the contact center to receive support.	Same as the above – companies can use customer inspiration, motivation, and education as actions to address feedback	FAQ sections on websites Product manuals	The company monitors the usage patterns on the customer level and identifies/predicts what the customer is trying to accomplish or whether they are using the product/service in a suboptimal fashion. It can then proactively contact them to support them in their efforts.

Who is doing it?	The vast majority of companies	Commonplace, typically indicates a strong customer-centric culture. Companies as different as Philips and Generali on one hand, and my local grocery delivery company or my barber shop have implemented some form of close-the-loop programs.	The vast majority of companies, especially those manufacturing products. Less common in service domains, albeit still available (in financial services, for example)	• Liberty Global, predicting customer dissatisfaction and contacting customers to prevent them from switching. • Garmin, offering customized training plans to people using their sport watches. • Adobe, with the training it provides in its Lightroom product. • Oral-B, with its application for electric toothbrush users, offering "personalized instructions, tips, and encouragement". (https://www.oralb.co.uk/en-gb/product-collections/oral-b-app)

Index

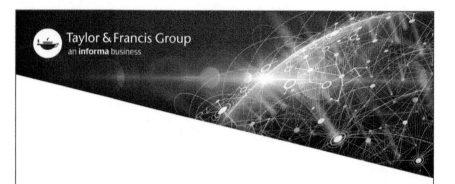